THE PLAN OF SALVATION

Books
by David J. Ridges

The *Gospel Studies Series:*

- *Isaiah Made Easier*
- *The New Testament Made Easier, Part 1*
- *The New Testament Made Easier, Part 2*
- *Your Study of The Book of Mormon Made Easier, Part 1*
- *Your Study of The Book of Mormon Made Easier, Part 2*
- *Your Study of The Book of Mormon Made Easier, Part 3*
- *Your Study of The Doctrine and Covenants Made Easier, Part 1*

Upcoming volumes in the *Gospel Studies Series*:

- *Your Study of The Doctrine and Covenants Made Easier, Part 2* (May 2005)
- *Your Study of The Doctrine and Covenants Made Easier, Part 3* (August 2005)
- *Your Study of The Pearl of Great Price Made Easier* (2005)
- *The Old Testament Made Easier—Selections from the Old Testament* (2006)

Additional titles by David J. Ridges:

- *The Proclamation on the Family: The Word of the Lord on More Than 30 Current Issues*
- *50 Signs of the Times and the Second Coming*

Doctrinal Details of the Plan of Salvation
From Premortality to Exaltation

David J. Ridges

CFI
Springville, Utah

ISBN: 1-55517-830-8
v.1

Published Cedar Fort, Inc.
925 N. Main Springville, UT, 84663
www.cedarfort.com

Distributed by:

Cover design by Nicole Williams
Cover design © 2005 by Lyle Mortimer

Printed in the United States of America
10 9 8 7 6 5 4 3 2 1

Printed on acid-free paper

DEDICATION

To my mother, Verla Nelson Ridges, who taught me to love the doctrines of the Plan of Salvation at an early age.

TABLE OF CONTENTS

PREFACE

G reat value comes from having the big picture of the Plan of Salvation in mind as we pursue our journey through this mortal life. The "plan of salvation" (Alma 42:5), or "great plan of happiness" (Alma 42:8), is the big picture. It is our Father's plan for providing the growth and development necessary for us to become like Him, to become gods and create our own worlds for our own spirit children. It is the plan that brings the highest joy, happiness, and satisfaction during the journey, as well as in the eternities.

This book is designed to be simple and to the point. It provides many of the doctrinal details of the Plan of Salvation. As we proceed, we will use the following simple chart to illustrate various stages of the Plan of Salvation:

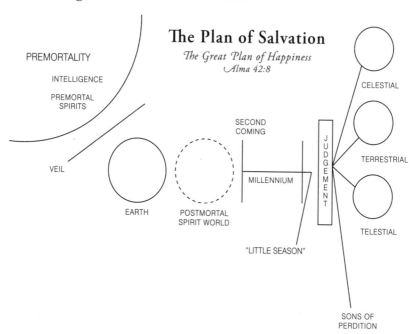

The Plan of Salvation
The Great Plan of Happiness
Alma 42:8

PREMORTALITY

INTELLIGENCE

PREMORTAL SPIRITS

VEIL

EARTH

POSTMORTAL SPIRIT WORLD

SECOND COMING

MILLENNIUM

"LITTLE SEASON"

JUDGEMENT

CELESTIAL

TERRESTRIAL

TELESTIAL

SONS OF PERDITION

As you can see, the chart illustrates the various stages of our progression and development, from premortality to the final Judgment Day and our assignment to one of the three degrees of glory or outer darkness. We will place a check mark (√) on the chart each time we use it to designate which portion of the Plan of Salvation we are discussing.

INTRODUCTION

In Doctrine and Covenants 10:62–63, the Savior stresses the importance of His "points of doctrine." The doctrines of the Plan of Salvation can serve as anchor points along the way as we journey through life. If we understand these doctrines, we are much more likely to make wise and correct decisions that affect our mortal probation—in both good times and bad times—as well as our eternal well-being.

Bold type is used throughout this book to emphasize important "points of doctrine." Brackets are used within quotes and scriptural verses to indicate comments by the author.

CHAPTER ONE

PRETEST

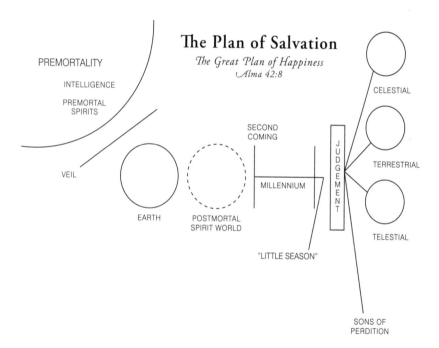

The Plan of Salvation
The Great Plan of Happiness
Alma 42:8

PREMORTALITY

INTELLIGENCE

PREMORTAL
SPIRITS

VEIL

EARTH

POSTMORTAL
SPIRIT WORLD

SECOND
COMING

MILLENNIUM

"LITTLE SEASON"

JUDGEMENT

CELESTIAL

TERRESTRIAL

TELESTIAL

SONS OF
PERDITION

Before beginning your study of the Plan of Salvation in this book, you may enjoy the challenge of taking the following pretest, which is given in the form of a true-false quiz. It deals with a number of doctrinal matters along the journey from premortality to final judgment and, for the righteous, exaltation. It can help you discover what you know and what you need to learn concerning the doctrines of the Plan of Salvation. While the quiz is not comprehensive, it covers many of the basics. We will also include an answer key. Some of the questions are purposely tricky to make you think.

One approach to using this book is to go ahead and take the whole pretest and then check your answers using the answer key. Another approach is to browse the pretest until you see something you would like to learn more about and then go to that question in the Answer Key for a brief answer.

Plan of Salvation Pretest

True or False

1. T F Most Christian churches don't teach premortal life as a doctrine.

2. T F As spirits in premortality, we were actual individuals but without physical bodies.

3. T F You first came into existence when you became a spirit child of Heavenly Parents.

4. T F You have always existed as intelligence and never did come into existence.

5. T F In premortality, our Heavenly Parents had resurrected, celestial bodies of flesh and bones.

6. T F Resurrected bodies produce spirit offspring.

7. T F You were actually born as a spirit child to Heavenly Parents.

8. T F Your spirit has always existed.

9. T F Spirit is actually a type of matter.

10. T F Spirit bodies have the same body parts that earthly physical bodies have.

11. T F Satan was the second oldest spirit (Christ was the oldest) in the premortal life.

12. T F We all developed equally in the premortal life because we were all in the presence of God.

13. T F During the War in Heaven, some spirits "sat on the fence"; that is to say, they couldn't decide whose side to be on.

14. T F Many spirits were killed in the War in Heaven.

15. T F In the council that preceded the War in Heaven, Jesus presented His plan and Lucifer presented his plan.

16. T F Some faithful people in the premortal life helped create the earth.

17. T F Satan and the one-third who followed him were cast down to earth and are still here today, tempting us.

18. T F Satan and the spirits who followed him are not only allowed to tempt us here on earth but also to tempt us after we die and go to the spirit world.

19. T F We have not yet been told where the postmortal spirit world is.

20. T F The spirit world is divided into two main categories: paradise and prison.

21. T F Only baptized, faithful members of the Church are allowed to enter paradise.

22. T F As wicked people die and enter the prison portion of the spirit world, they find out that life continues after mortal death and therefore immediately want missionaries there to preach the gospel to them.

23. T F The "veil" over our minds prevents us from remembering our premortal life.

24. T F The veil is removed when people die and go to the spirit world.

25. T F There were male spirits and female spirits in our premortal life.

26. T F When babies are born here on earth, they have full-grown spirits in them.

27. T F On rare occasions, when a child who has died is permitted to appear to someone to provide comfort or whatever, it can appear as a child or as a full-grown spirit, or whatever age is appropriate for the occasion.

28. T F Without this earth life, we could never be exalted.

29. T F After the final Judgment Day, everyone but exalted people will be single.

30. T F In the next life, only those who attain celestial exaltation will have use of the powers of procreation and live in the family unit.

31. T F Those who achieve exaltation will actually be making and peopling worlds of their own.

32. T F Because exaltation is extremely difficult to attain, few will actually attain it.

33. T F Christ will wear red when He comes, representing His blood that was shed for the righteous.

34. T F The "morning of the first resurrection" refers to people who will be resurrected when Christ comes at the Second Coming and will achieve celestial glory.

35. T F No significant differences will exist between the resurrected bodies of celestial people and those of terrestrial and telestial people because their bodies will all be perfect.

36. T F No telestial people have been resurrected yet.

37. T F We don't know how long people will live during the Millennium.

38. T F There will be no wicked people during the Millennium.

39. T F Satan will be around, trying to tempt people during the Millennium, but nobody will listen to him.

40. T F People living during the Millennium will still be mortal.

41. T F Babies who died before the age of accountability and people who are born during the Millennium will be tested when Satan is let loose at the end of the Millennium.

42. T F Christ and the resurrected Saints will reign over the earth during the Millennium but will not necessarily dwell here.

43. T F Heavenly Father will be our final judge.

44. T F Those who become gods will use the same Plan of Salvation as is used for us, for their own spirit children.

Answer Key

Answers (T=true, F=false, ?=it depends, or we don't know)

1. **?** Jeremiah 1:5 clearly teaches premortal life, but few, if any, Christian churches teach it as a formal doctrine. Therefore, you could have answered True. However, many Christians, as well as other people, do believe in a life with God before this earth life. Also, members of many non-Christian religions believe in a life, or lives, before this one. Therefore, you could have answered false.

2. **T** True. Many people don't realize that we were real, thinking, acting, individuals there (see Abraham 3:18–24).

3. **F** "There is something called intelligence which has always existed. It is the real eternal part of man, which was not created or made" (Joseph Fielding Smith, *The Progress of Man*, 10; see also D&C 93:29). The Prophet Joseph Smith said, "The intelligence of spirits had no beginning" (*History of the Church*, 6:311). The Prophet taught clearly that man is the offspring of God and that the spirits of men were born in the spirit world as the children of God (see *Teachings of the Prophet Joseph Smith*, 158, footnote 5; see also 352–53).

4. **T** See 3 above. Elder John A. Widtsoe said, "The eternal ego of man was, in some past age of the other world, dim to us, clothed with a spiritual body. That was man's spiritual birth and his entrance into the spiritual world. Then later, on earth, . . . he will receive a material body. The term *an intelligence* is then applied to the eternal ego existing even before the spiritual creation. In reading latter-day literature, the two-fold sense in which the terms *an intelligence or intelligences* are used—applied to spiritual personages or to pre-spiritual entities—must be carefully kept in mind (*Evidences and Reconciliations*, 3:74–77, 1951).

5. **T** "The Father has a body of flesh and bones" (D&C 130:22). We understand from the following quote that both Heavenly Father and Heavenly Mother have glorified resurrected bodies of flesh and bone. "Only resurrected and glorified beings can become parents of spirit offspring. Only such exalted souls have reached maturity in the appointed course of eternal life; and the spirits born to them in the eternal worlds will pass in due sequence through the several stages or estates by which the glorified parents have attained exaltation" (Joseph F. Smith, *Gospel Doctrine*, 70).

6. **?** This could be either true or false, depending on how technical you get. It is true, in a general sense, that resurrected bodies produce spirit offspring (see 5 above); however, only those in the highest degree of the celestial kingdom will use the powers of procreation to bring forth spirit children (see D&C 131:1–4). Joseph Fielding Smith taught, "Some of the functions in the celestial body will not appear in the terrestrial body, neither in the telestial body, and *the power of procreation will be removed*" (*Doctrines of Salvation*, 2:288).

7. **T** "We are also his offspring. . . . We are the offspring of God" (Acts 17:28–29). As members of the First Presidency, President Joseph F. Smith, John R. Winder, and Anthon H. Lund said, "All men and women are in the similitude of the universal Father and Mother, and are literally the sons and daughters of Deity" (Clark, *Messages of the First Presidency*, 4:203).

   In *Mormon Doctrine*, under "Birth," we read, "All men were first born in pre-existence as the literal *spirit offspring* of God our Heavenly Father. . . . By the ordained procreative process our exalted and immortal Father begat his spirit progeny in pre-existence. . . . When the spirit children of the Father pass from his presence into this mortal sphere, a *mortal birth* results. Again by the ordained pro-creative process a body is provided" (McConkie, *Mormon Doctrine*, 84).

The First Presidency (President Heber J. Grant and his counselors,) said, "Man, as a spirit, was begotten and born of heavenly parents, and reared to maturity in the eternal mansions of the Father, prior to coming upon the earth" ("The Mormon View of Evolution," *Improvement Era*, September 1925).

8. **T** See 3 above. If you want to be technical, you could say this is true in the sense that spirit is matter (D&C 131:7–8), and so the matter from which your spirit body was created has always existed.

9. **T** See Doctrine and Covenants 131:7–8.

10. **T** See Ether 3:6, where the brother of Jared sees "the finger of the Lord," which "was as the finger of a man, like unto flesh and blood," and Ether 3:16, where the premortal Christ told him that he was seeing "the body of my spirit."

"Our *spirit bodies* had their beginning in pre-existence when we were born as the spirit children of God our Father. . . . The bodies so created have all the parts of mortal bodies" (McConkie, *Mormon Doctrine*, 750).

A quote from the *Doctrines of the Gospel Student Manual*, page 14, is also helpful: "It [the spirit body] possesses, in fact, all the organs and parts exactly corresponding to the outward tabernacle" [i.e., physical body].

11. **F** This rumor has been around for a long time. It is not documented by authoritative sources and therefore must be considered false. This rumor may come from people's interpretation of scriptures such as Isaiah 14:12, where

Satan is referred to as "Lucifer, son of the morning." Doctrine and Covenants 76:26 refers to Satan as "a" son of the morning, not "the" son of the morning. Or people might be reading Abraham 3:28, where it says "the second (Satan) was angry," meaning the second one to volunteer to be our redeemer, not the second one to be born. So we don't know when Satan was born into the premortal spirit world.

12. **F** We know that we developed at different rates. The Savior is our Elder Brother and is far ahead of us. Also, obvious differences show up in us as we come through the veil into mortality (see Abraham 3:19, 22; Alma 13).

13. **F** "There were no neutrals in the war in heaven. *All took sides either with Christ or with Satan*" (Smith, *Doctrines of Salvation*, 1:65–66). Obviously, some may have taken longer to make up their minds whom to follow, but ultimately we all had to choose.

14. **F** Spirits cannot be killed. It was a war of words, philosophies, true and false doctrines, and so forth. The war is still going on here on earth. Of course, you could have answered true if you were thinking of spiritual death—being cast out with Satan and permanently cut off from the presence of God (see D&C 29:41; Helaman 14:18; Alma 12:16).

15. **F** A careful reading of Moses 4:1–3 shows that just one plan was presented. It was the Father's plan. Jehovah (Christ) sustained Heavenly Father's plan, saying, "Thy will be done." Satan had the arrogance to attempt to amend or modify the Father's perfect plan, saying, "I will be thy son, and I will redeem all mankind, that one soul shall not be lost, and surely I will do it; wherefore give me thine honor. . . . [He] sought to destroy the agency of man, which I, the Lord God, had given him."

16. **T** See Abraham 3:22–24. Joseph Fielding Smith said, "It is true that Adam helped to form this earth. He labored with our Savior Jesus Christ. I have a strong view or conviction that there were others also who assisted them. Perhaps Noah and Enoch; and *why not Joseph Smith*, and those who were appointed to be rulers before the earth was formed?" (*Doctrines of Salvation*, 1:74–75).

17. **T** See Revelation 12:4, 7–9; 2 Nephi 9:9, and D&C 29:36–39.

18. **?** You could answer either way, depending on your thinking. It is true that Satan and his evil spirits can tempt people in the spirit world, but *only* in the prison portion. "When the righteous saints go to paradise, they will no longer be tempted, but the wicked in hell are subject to the control and torments of Lucifer" (McConkie, *Mormon Doctrine*, 782; see also *Teachings of the Presidents of the Church—Brigham Young*, 282).

19. **F** "That [spirit] world is upon this earth" (McConkie, *Mormon Doctrine*, 762, quoting from *Teachings of the Prophet Joseph Smith*, 326, and *Discourses of Brigham Young*, 376).

20. **T** See Alma 40:11–14 and 1 Peter 3:18–19.

21. **?** It depends on how technical you want to be in answering this question. In the general sense, it is true. However, all children who die before the years of accountability obviously go to paradise. Therefore, you could answer false. As far as all others are concerned, Joseph Fielding Smith, speaking of the spirit world, said, "There, as I understand it, *the righteous—meaning those who have been baptized and who have been faithful—*are gathered in one part and all the others in another part. . . . The unrighteous . . . *included all the spirits not baptized*" (*Doctrines of Salvation*, 2:230; see also *Teachings of the Presidents of the Church—*

Brigham Young, 282).

22. **F** Alma 34:34 tells us that people will still be basically the same when they enter the spirit world, so "instant conversions" probably won't happen very often.

23. **T** Joseph Fielding Smith taught the following: "In our former, or spirit existence, we walked by sight. We were in the presence of both the Father and the Son, and were instructed by them and under their personal presence. In this mortal life, or second estate, the Lord willed that we should walk by faith and not by sight, that we might, with the great gift of free agency, be proved to see if we would do all things whatsoever the Lord our God commanded us. Therefore, he took away from us all knowledge of our spiritual existence and started us out afresh in the form of helpless infants, to grow and learn day by day. In consequence of this we received no former knowledge and wisdom at birth, and, as it is written of the Son of God, who in the beginning made all things, we 'received not of the fulness at the first, but received grace for grace'" (*Doctrines of Salvation,* 1:60).

24. **?** We don't yet know the answer for sure. We do know that those in the spirit prison don't get their memory of premortality back; they are in "darkness" and must have the gospel preached to them (D&C 138:30–32). But obviously, Abraham, Isaac, and Jacob have their memories of premortality because they have already become gods (D&C 132:37). We simply don't know exactly when people in paradise will get their memories back.

25. **T** In "The Family: A Proclamation to the World," the First Presidency and Quorum of the Twelve Apostles declared, "All human beings—male and female—are created in the image of God. Each is a beloved spirit son or daughter of heavenly parents" (*Ensign,* November 1995, 102). Earlier,

the First Presidency taught, "All men and women are in the similitude of the universal Father and Mother, and are literally the sons and daughters of Deity" (Clark, *Messages of the First Presidency,* 4:203).

Bruce R. McConkie taught, "These spirit beings, the off-spring of exalted parents, were men and women, appearing in all respects as mortal persons do, excepting only that their spirit bodies were made of a more pure and refined substance than the elements from which mortal bodies are made" (*Mormon Doctrine,* 589; see also 1 Nephi 11:11; Ether 3:16).

26. **T** President Joseph F. Smith said in 1918, "The Spirit of Jesus Christ was full-grown before he was born into the world; and so our children were full-grown and possessed their full stature in the spirit, before they entered mortality, the same stature that they will possess after they have passed away from mortality, and as they will also appear after the resurrection, when they shall have completed their mission" (*Gospel Doctrine,* 455).

27. **T** "If you see one of your children that has passed away it may appear to you in the form in which you would recognize it, the form of childhood; but if it came to you as a messenger bearing some important truth, it would perhaps come as the spirit of Bishop Edward Hunter's son (who died when he was a little child) came to him, in the stature of full-grown manhood, and revealed himself to his father, and said: 'I am your son'" (Smith, *Gospel Doctrine,* 455).

28. **T** "The mortal estate in which we find ourselves is absolutely necessary to our exaltation" (Smith, *Doctrines of Salvation,* 1:91).

29. **T** See D&C 131:1–4; 132:16–17. Referring to those who go to the terrestrial and telestial kingdoms, Joseph Fielding

Smith said, "*In both of these kingdoms there will be changes in the bodies and limitations. They will not have the power of increase, neither the power or nature to live as husbands and wives, for this will be denied them and they cannot increase.* Those who receive the exaltation in the celestial kingdom will have the 'continuation of the seeds forever' [D&C 132:19]. *They will live in the family relationship.* In the terrestrial and in the telestial kingdoms there will be no marriage. Those who enter there will remain 'separately and singly' forever" (*Doctrines of Salvation*, 2:287).

30. **T** "*Some will gain celestial bodies with all the powers of exaltation and eternal increase*," Joseph Fielding Smith said. Referring to the terrestrial and telestial kingdoms, he added, "*There will be changes in the bodies and limitations. They will not have the power of increase, neither the power or nature to live as husbands and wives, for this will be denied them and they cannot increase*" (*Doctrines of Salvation*, 2: 287; see also D&C 131:1–4).

31. **T** See D&C 132:20, 22. President Brigham Young said, "After men have got their exaltations and their crowns—have become Gods . . . they have the power then of propagating their species in spirit; and that is the first of their operations with regard to organizing a world" (in *Journal of Discourses*, 6:275).

32. **F** Innumerable people will be exalted (D&C 76:67; Revelation 7:9).

33. **F** He will wear red (Isaiah 63:2; D&C 133:48), but the color will represent the blood of the wicked, who will be destroyed at His coming (D&C 133:51).

34. **?** This term is not used in the scriptures, but it is used in modern LDS vocabulary. It is sometimes used in patriarchal blessings and generally refers to the righteous, who will be resurrected when the Savior comes for the Second

Coming. It can also simply refer to all those who are resurrected with celestial bodies and thus will enter celestial glory.

Those whose patriarchal blessings say something to the effect that they will come forth on the morning of the first resurrection do not necessarily have to have died by the time of the Second Coming. For them, the "morning" could easily mean *during* the Millennium, after they have lived out their mortal years. Thus, the answer to this question is true for the righteous who have already died by the time Christ comes. The righteous who are still living when He comes will be taken up to meet Him (D&C 88:96) and will then continue to live on earth until they die. Then they will be resurrected as part of the "morning of the first resurrection," or celestial resurrection.

In the *Doctrines of the Gospel Student Manual*, pages 88–89, an explanation of the term "morning of the first resurrection" is given in the context of the order in which the righteous and wicked will be resurrected:

"Two great resurrections await the inhabitants of the earth: one is the *first resurrection, the resurrection of life, the resurrection of the just;* the other is the *second resurrection, the resurrection of damnation, the resurrection of the unjust* (John 5:28–29; Rev. 20; D&C 76.) But even within these two separate resurrections, there is an order in which the dead will come forth. Those being resurrected with celestial bodies, whose destiny is to inherit a celestial kingdom, will come forth in the **morning of the first resurrection.** . . .

"'And after this another angel shall sound, which is the second trump; and then cometh the redemption of those who are Christ's at his coming; who have received their part in that prison which is prepared for them, that they might receive the gospel, and be judged according to men in the flesh.' (D&C 88:99.) This is the *afternoon* of the first resurrection; it takes place after our Lord has ushered in the millennium. Those coming forth at that time do so with terrestrial bodies and are thus destined to inherit a terrestrial glory in eternity. (D&C 76:71–80.)

"At the end of the millennium, the second resurrection begins. In the forepart of this resurrection of the unjust those destined to come forth will be 'the spirits of men who are to be judged, and are found under condemnation; and these are the rest of the dead; and they live not again until the thousand years are ended, neither again, until the end of the earth.' (D&C 88:100–101.) These are the ones who have earned telestial bodies, who were wicked and carnal in mortality, and who have suffered the wrath of God in hell 'until the last resurrection, until the Lord, even Christ the Lamb, shall have finished his work.' (D&C 76:85.) Their final destiny is to inherit a telestial glory. (D&C 76:81–112.)

"Finally, in the latter end of the resurrection of damnation, the sons of perdition, those who 'remain filthy still' (D&C 88:102), shall come forth from their graves. (2 Ne. 9:14–16.)" (McConkie, *Mormon Doctrine*, 640; see also *Doctrines of the Gospel Student Manual*, 88–89).

35. **F** "In the resurrection there will be different kinds of bodies; they will not all be alike. The body a man receives will determine his place hereafter. There will be celestial bodies, terrestrial bodies, and telestial bodies, and these bodies will differ" (Smith, *Doctrines of Salvation*, 2:286; see also 1 Corinthians 15:39–42; D&C 88:28–32; and answers 29 and 30 above).

36. **T** Telestial people will not be resurrected until the end of the Millennium (D&C 88:100–101).

37. **F** Isaiah 65:20 says people will live to be one hundred years old. Joseph Fielding Smith, speaking of life during the

Millennium, said, "A change, nevertheless, will come over all who remain on the earth; they will be quickened so that they will not be subject unto death until they are old. Men shall die when they are one hundred years of age" (*Way to Perfection,* 298–99; see also *Doctrines of the Gospel Student Manual,* 104).

38. **?** The answer depends on how specific you want to be. Obviously, at the beginning of the Millennium, there will be no wicked because they will have been destroyed. The Millennium will be a time of peace. However, Isaiah 65:20 indicates that there will be an occasional sinner during the Millennium who will be accursed at the end of his hundred years.

39. **F** Regarding the binding of Satan during the Millennium, Joseph Fielding Smith taught, "There are many among us who teach that the binding of Satan will be merely the binding which those dwelling on the earth will place upon him by their refusal to hear his enticings. This is not so. He will not have the privilege during that period of time to tempt any man (D&C 101:28)" (*Church History and Modern Revelation,* 1:192; see also *Doctrine and Covenants Student Manual,* 89).

40. **T** "Physical bodies of those living on earth during the millennium will not be subject to the same ills that attend us in our present sphere of existence. Men in that day will still be mortal. . . . But their bodies will be changed from conditions as they now exist so that disease cannot attack them, and death as we know it cannot intervene to cause a separation of body and spirit" (McConkie, *Mormon Doctrine,* 497–98).

41. **F** This is false doctrine that keeps floating around. D&C 137:10 tells us that children who die before the age of accountability "are saved in the celestial kingdom of heaven."

People who live during the Millennium will live to be a hundred and will then be "twinkled"—resurrected into a body that represents the kingdom that they will receive (Isaiah 65:20; see also D&C 88:28–32).

42. **T** The Prophet Joseph Smith said, "Christ and the resurrected Saints will reign over the earth during the thousand years. They will not probably dwell upon the earth, but will visit it when they please, or when it is necessary to govern it" (*Teachings of the Prophet Joseph Smith*, 268).

43. **F** The Bible teaches that the Father has instructed the Son to be our final judge. "The Father judgeth no man, but hath committed all judgment unto the Son" (John 5:22).

44. **T** In 1916, the First Presidency said, "Only resurrected and glorified beings can become parents of spirit offspring. Only such exalted souls have reached maturity in the appointed course of eternal life; and the spirits born to them in the eternal worlds will pass in due sequence through the several stages or estates by which the glorified parents have attained exaltation" (1916 First Presidency Statement, *Improvement Era*, August 1916, 942).

Having taken the above true-false quiz and thus reviewed some of the doctrines of the Plan of Salvation, we will now begin our more detailed study in chapter two, next, as we consider our pre-earth life.

PREMORTALITY

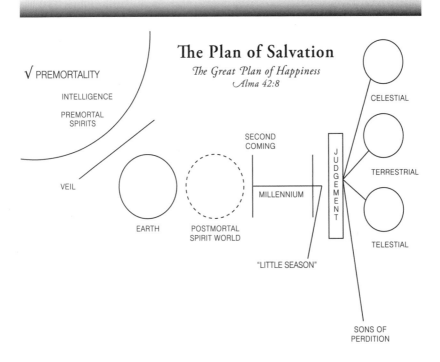

The Plan of Salvation

The Great Plan of Happiness
Alma 42:8

√ PREMORTALITY

INTELLIGENCE

PREMORTAL SPIRITS

VEIL

EARTH

POSTMORTAL SPIRIT WORLD

SECOND COMING

MILLENNIUM

"LITTLE SEASON"

JUDGEMENT

CELESTIAL

TERRESTRIAL

TELESTIAL

SONS OF PERDITION

*P**remortality* refers to our existence before we came to earth to live. As you can see on the above chart, there were two phases or stages of our existence there: intelligence and premortal spirits.

Satan has done much to eliminate the concept or belief in a premortal existence as a basic doctrine in the teachings of most Christian religions. Yet, in the hearts of many individuals, there is a belief or quiet feeling that they came from God and that there is life after death. Many non-Christian religions teach reincarnation—the belief that we did have a life, or several lives, before this one, and that we lived as a person of a lower or higher caste or as an animal, a plant, and so forth. In this belief system, people will return as either more-favored or less-favored individuals, depending on their behavior in this life. This cycle of reincarnation continues until people learn and grow to the point of being accepted into heaven (there are various terms for this).

Though there is no such thing as reincarnation (Hebrews 9:27 tells us that we live only once), these non-Christian religions at least teach that this life is not the beginning of our existence. Many Christian religions lack such a doctrine in their formal teachings.

When you think about it, it becomes obvious why Satan has put such effort into eliminating both the concept of pre-earth life and life after death. If neither one exists, then what is the purpose of life? We are nothing but a biological accident on a meaningless planet among countless specks in space. There is no reason for living, no accountability, no basic worth. If the devil can promote these false doctrines, he succeeds in promoting a philosophy of worthlessness, lack of responsibility, disrespect for self and others, and ultimately, gloom and depression.

The true gospel of Jesus Christ teaches just the opposite. It teaches bright hope through the Atonement of Christ. It illuminates the eternal nature of mankind, the infinite worth of the soul, and the value of the quest for personal righteousness and the selfless serving of others. Thus, the "plan of salvation" (Alma 42:5), which we are studying in this book, is also referred to as "the great plan of happiness" (Alma 42:8). We will now take a closer look at our life before we were born into mortality.

The pre-earth stage of our existence is often referred to as "pre-existence." Perhaps you've noticed that the Church is tending to not use that term anymore. One of the reasons is that it can be confusing to people who are unfamiliar with the gospel and the Plan of Salvation. When we speak of what we did in the "pre-existence," people wonder how we could do things before we existed. To them, it is a contradiction in terms. Thus, we now use such terms as premortal life, premortality, premortal existence, pre-earth life, and so forth in our gospel conversations.

The basic part of our being, referred to as either "intelligence" or "intelligences," has existed forever. We came into existence as spirits when we were born as a "spirit son or daughter of heavenly parents" ("The Family: A Proclamation to the World," *Ensign*, November 1995, 102).

As we proceed, we will ask some questions about our premortal existence and provide answers from the scriptures and the teachings of Church leaders. **Bolding** is used for emphasis in citations of the scriptures and teachings.

Premortal Existence—As Intelligence

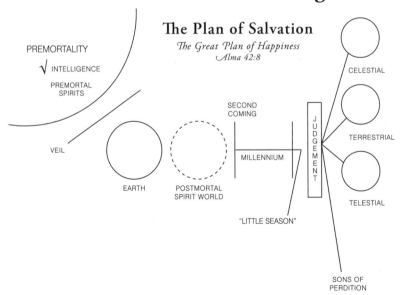

The Plan of Salvation
The Great Plan of Happiness
Alma 42:8

PREMORTALITY

√ INTELLIGENCE

PREMORTAL SPIRITS

VEIL

EARTH

POSTMORTAL SPIRIT WORLD

SECOND COMING

MILLENNIUM

"LITTLE SEASON"

JUDGEMENT

CELESTIAL

TERRESTRIAL

TELESTIAL

SONS OF PERDITION

Q: How long did we exist as intelligence?

A: We have existed as "intelligence" or "intelligences" forever.

Doctrine and Covenants 93:29

"Intelligence, or the light of truth, was not created or made, neither indeed can be."

Joseph Smith

"Is it logical to say that the intelligence of spirits is immortal, and yet that it has a beginning? The intelligence of spirits had no beginning, neither will it have an end. . . . Intelligence is eternal and exists upon a self-existent principle" (*History of the Church* 6:311).

Q: Do we know what intelligence is?

A: No.

Notice in the quote below that Joseph Fielding Smith (an apostle who became the tenth president of the Church) did not know for sure which word to use for the first stage of our premortal existence.

Joseph Fielding Smith

"The intelligent part of man was not created, but always existed. There has been some speculation and articles have been written attempting to explain just what these '**intelligences**' are, or this '**intelligence**' is, but it is futile for us to speculate upon it. We do know that intelligence was not created or made and cannot be because the Lord has said it. There are some truths it is well to leave until the Lord sees fit to reveal the fulness" (*Church History and Modern Revelation*, 1:401).

Here is a similar quote, also from Joseph Fielding Smith, followed by a quote from Elder John A. Widtsoe on the subject of "intelligence."

Joseph Fielding Smith

"Some of our writers have endeavored to explain what an intelligence is, but to do so is futile, for we have never been given any insight into this matter beyond what the Lord has fragmentarily revealed. We know, however, that **there is something called intelligence which has always existed.** It is the real eternal part of man, which was not created or made. **This intelligence combined with the spirit constitutes a spiritual identity or individual**" (*Progress of Man*, 10).

John A. Widtsoe

"Under this concept, **the eternal ego** [intelligence] **of man was,** in some past age of the other world, dim to us, **clothed with a spiritual body.** That was man's **spiritual birth and his entrance into the spiritual world.** Then later, on earth, if permitted to go there, he will receive a material body. As a result, after the resurrection he will be master of the things of the spiritual and material universes, and in that manner approach the likeness of God.

"This view of the nature of man is a widespread belief among Latter-day Saints. **The term** *an intelligence* **is then applied to the external ego existing even before the spiritual creation.**

"In reading Latter-day Saint literature, the two-fold sense in which the terms *an intelligence* or *intelligences* are used—applied to spiritual personages or to pre-spiritual entities—must be carefully kept in mind" (*Evidences and Reconciliations*, 3:74–77).

Q: Are the words "intelligence" and "spirit" sometimes used interchangeably?

A: Yes.

This can be a bit confusing. Perhaps you've noticed that some gospel vocabulary words are very context sensitive. "Soul" is one such gospel term used to mean different things, depending on the context.

In some contexts or scriptural settings, "soul" can mean "spirit." (After she died, her "soul" went to heaven.) In another context, it can mean "center of feelings." (He felt the truth of the gospel deep within his "soul.") Doctrine and Covenants 88:15, however, gives us a basic gospel doctrinal definition of the word: "The **spirit** and the **body** are **the soul** of man."

Now, back to the terms "intelligence" and "spirit." Scriptural use of the terms "intelligence" and "spirit" is likewise context sensitive. For example, in one part of the book of Abraham, "intelligences" means "spirits"; in another context within the same chapter, it means "intelligence." This can be a bit confusing unless we pay close attention to context. Let's take a closer look.

Abraham 3:18–22

18 Howbeit that he made the greater star; as, also, if there be two **spirits,** and one shall be more intelligent than the other, yet these two **spirits,** notwithstanding one is more intelligent than the other, **have no beginning** [intelligence has no beginning; see D&C 93:29]; they existed before, **they shall have no end,** they shall exist after, for they are gnolaum, or eternal.

21 I dwell in the midst of them all; I now, therefore, have come down unto thee to declare unto thee the works which my hands have made, wherein my wisdom excelleth them all, for I rule in the heavens above, and in the earth beneath, in all wisdom and prudence, over all the intelligences [spirits] thine eyes have seen from the beginning; I came down in the beginning [meaning in the

premortal council among the spirits] in the midst of all the **intelligences** [spirits] thou hast seen.

22 Now the Lord had shown unto me, Abraham, the **intelligences** [spirits] that were organized before the world was; and among all these there were many of the noble and great ones."

Joseph Fielding Smith explained that "the beginning," as used in verse 21 above, refers to our existence as spirits at the time the councils were held and our opportunity to come to earth was explained to us.

Joseph Fielding Smith

"The Lord made it known to Moses [see Moses 3] and also to Abraham [see Abraham 3] and it is expressed in several revelations, that **man was in the beginning with God. In that day,** however, **man was a spirit** unembodied. **The beginning was when the councils met and the decision was made to create this earth that the spirits who were intended for this earth, should come here and partake of the mortal conditions and receive bodies of flesh and bones.** The doctrine has prevailed that matter was created out of nothing, but the Lord declares that the elements are eternal. Matter always did and, therefore, always will exist, and the spirits of men as well as their bodies were created out of matter" (*Church History and Modern Revelation,* 1:401; see also *Doctrines of the Gospel Student Manual,* 13).

We know little about intelligence, or intelligences, other than the fact that we did exist as such, forever, before we were born as spirit children of our Father in Heaven. We will now move on to the next stage of our premortal existence, namely, as spirits. We have much more information about this stage.

Premortal Existence—As Spirits

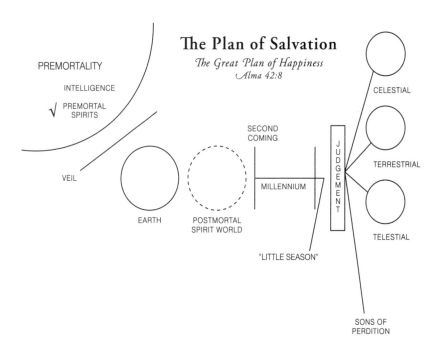

The Plan of Salvation
The Great Plan of Happiness
Alma 42:8

PREMORTALITY

INTELLIGENCE

PREMORTAL SPIRITS

VEIL

EARTH

POSTMORTAL SPIRIT WORLD

SECOND COMING

MILLENNIUM

"LITTLE SEASON"

JUDGEMENT

CELESTIAL

TERRESTRIAL

TELESTIAL

SONS OF PERDITION

We began our life as premortal spirits when we were born to our Heavenly Parents. At that point, our intelligence was clothed with a spirit body. Elder Widtsoe, as previously quoted, taught this truth:

John A. Widtsoe
"**The eternal ego** [intelligence] of man was, in some past age of the other world, dim to us, **clothed with a spiritual body.** That was man's **spiritual birth and his entrance into the spiritual world**" (*Evidences and Reconciliations,* 3:74–77).

Q: Would it be correct to say that our Heavenly Parents gave our intelligence a spirit body?

A: Yes.

President Spencer W. Kimball explained this fact:

Spencer W. Kimball
"God is your father. He loves you. **He and your mother in heaven** value you beyond any measure. They **gave your eternal intelligence spirit form, just as your earthly mother and father have given you a mortal body.** You are unique. One of a kind, made of the eternal intelligence which gives you claim upon eternal life.

"Let there be no question in your mind about your value as an individual. The whole intent of the gospel plan is to provide an opportunity for each of you to reach your fullest potential, which is eternal progression and the possibility of godhood" ("Privileges and Responsibilities of Sisters," *Ensign,* November 1978, 105).

Q: Am I really a "child of God"? Were we actually "born" as spirit children to our Heavenly Parents?

A: Yes.

The Apostle Paul explains clearly in the Bible that we are the offspring of God. Perhaps you've noticed in your Bible reading that the word "create" is often used in reference to the creation of all things, including mankind. However, the word, "offspring" is used only in reference to human beings. In other words, we are literally the offspring or children of God! We will quote Paul and others on this subject:

Acts 17:28–29
"We are also his offspring. . . . **We are the offspring of God.**"

The First Presidency

"**All men and women** are in the similitude of the universal Father and Mother, and **are literally the sons and daughters of Deity**" (Clark, *Messages of the First Presidency,* 4:203; see also *Doctrines of the Gospel Student Manual,* 14).

"The Family—A Proclamation to the World"

"All human beings—male and female—are created in the image of God. **Each is a beloved spirit son or daughter of heavenly parents**" (*Ensign,* November 1995, 102).

Bruce R. McConkie

"All men were first **born in pre-existence as the literal *spirit offspring* of God** our Heavenly Father. . . . **By the ordained procreative process** our exalted immortal Father begat his spirit progeny in pre-existence. . . . When the spirit children of the Father pass from his presence into this mortal sphere, a *mortal birth* results. Again by the ordained procreative process a body is provided" (*Mormon Doctrine,* 84).

The First Presidency

"**Man, as a spirit,** was **begotten** [conceived] and **born** of **heavenly parents,** and **reared to maturity** in the eternal mansions of the Father, **prior to coming upon the earth**" ("The Mormon View of Evolution," *Improvement Era,* September, 1925.)

Q: Is spirit a form of actual matter?
A: Yes.

D&C 131:7–8

7 There is no such thing as immaterial matter. **All spirit is matter,** but it is more fine or pure, and can only be discerned by purer eyes;

8 We cannot see it; but when our bodies are purified we shall see that **it is all matter.**

Q: Do our spirit bodies have the same parts that our mortal bodies have? In other words, were we "real people" as spirits in premortality?

A: Yes.

D&C 77:2

2 **That which is spiritual** [the spirit] being **in the likeness of that which is temporal** [the physical body]; and that which is temporal in the likeness of that which is spiritual [the physical body is similar to the spirit body]; **the spirit of man in the likeness of his person,** as also the spirit of the beast [the spirits of animals look like their physical bodies], and every other creature which God has created.

Bruce R. McConkie

"Our *spirit bodies* had their beginning in pre-existence when we were born as the spirit children of God our Father. . . . **The bodies so created have all the parts of mortal bodies**" (*Mormon Doctrine,* 750).

Parley P. Pratt

"**The spirit of man** consists of an organization of the elements of spiritual matter in the likeness and after the pattern of the fleshly tabernacle [body]. It **possesses, in fact, all the organs and parts exactly corresponding to** the outward tabernacle [physical body]" (*Key to the Science of Theology*, 79; see also *Doctrines of the Gospel Student Manual*, 14).

Q: Do all forms of life have spirits?
A: Yes.

Moses 3:5, 9

5 And every plant of the field before it was in the earth, and every herb of the field before it grew. **For I, the Lord God, created all things, of which I have spoken, spiritually** [meaning, in this context, "in spirit form"], **before they were naturally upon the face of the earth.** For I, the Lord God, had not caused it to rain upon the face of the earth. And I, the Lord God, had created all the children of men; and not yet a man to till the ground; for **in heaven created I them;** and there was not yet flesh upon the earth, neither in the water, neither in the air;

9 And out of the ground made I, the Lord God, to grow every tree, naturally, that is pleasant to the sight of man; and man could behold it. And it became also a living soul. For **it was spiritual in the day that I created it;** for it remaineth in the sphere in which I, God, created it [meaning, among other things, that every living thing still has a spirit within its physical housing], yea, even all things which I prepared for the use of man; and man saw that it was good for food. And I, the Lord God, planted the tree of life also in the midst of the garden, and also the tree of knowledge of good and evil.

Bruce R. McConkie

"Man and **all forms of life existed as spirit beings and entities** before the foundations of this earth were laid. There were **spirit men** and **spirit beasts, spirit fowls** and

spirit fishes, spirit plants and **spirit trees.** Every **creeping thing,** every **herb** and **shrub,** every **amoeba** and **tadpole,** every **elephant** and **dinosaur**—all things—existed as spirits, as spirit beings, before they were placed naturally upon the earth" (*The Millennial Messiah,* 642–43; see *also Doctrines of the Gospel Student Manual,* 16).

Q: Did worthy men have priesthood in the premortal life?
A: Yes.

Alma 13:1–3

1 And again, my brethren, I would cite your minds forward to the time when the Lord God gave these commandments unto his children; and I would that ye should remember that **the Lord God ordained priests, after his holy order** [the Melchizedek Priesthood], which was after the order of his Son [the same priesthood held by Christ], to teach these things unto the people.

2 And **those priests were ordained after the order of his Son,** in a manner that thereby the people might know in what manner to look forward to his Son for redemption.

3 And this is the manner after which **they were** ordained—being **called and prepared from the foundation of the world** [in other words, in premortality] according to the foreknowledge of God, on account of their exceeding faith and good works; in the first place [in premortality] being left to choose good or evil; therefore they having chosen good, and exercising exceedingly great faith, are called with a holy calling, yea, with that holy calling which was prepared with, and according to, a preparatory redemption for such.

Bruce R. McConkie

"Alma says that those 'ordained unto the high priesthood of the holy order of God' were 'in the first place,' that is in pre-existence, 'on the same standing with their brethren,' meaning that initially all had equal opportunity to progress through righteousness. But while yet in the eternal worlds, certain of the offspring of God, 'having chosen good, and exercising exceeding great faith,' were as a consequence 'called and prepared from the foundation of the world according to the foreknowledge of God' to enjoy the blessings and powers of the priesthood. These priesthood calls were made 'from the foundation of the world,' or in other words faithful men held priesthood power and authority first in pre-existence and then again on earth. (Alma 13.) 'Every man who has a calling to minister to the inhabitants of the world was ordained to that very purpose in the Grand Council of heaven before this world was.' (*Teachings*, p. 365.)" (*Mormon Doctrine*, 477; see also *Book of Mormon Student Manual*, 1982, 237).

Joseph Fielding Smith

"It is reasonable to believe that there was a church organization there [in premortality]. . . . **Priesthood, without any question, had been conferred and the leaders were chosen to officiate. Ordinances pertaining to that pre-existence were required** and the love of God prevailed" (*Way to Perfection*, 50–51; see also *Doctrines of the Gospel Student Manual*, 14).

Q: Did the Atonement work for us in premortality also?

A: Yes. The following quote from Revelation, dealing with the War in Heaven, refers to the Atonement in premortality as well as mortality.

Revelation 12:7–11

7 And **there was war in heaven:** Michael and his angels fought against the dragon; and the dragon fought and his angels,

8 And prevailed not; neither was their place found any more in heaven.

9 And the great dragon was cast out, that old serpent, called the Devil, and **Satan,** which deceiveth the whole world: he **was cast out** into the earth, **and his angels were cast out with him.**

10 And I heard a loud voice saying in heaven, Now is come salvation, and strength, and the kingdom of our God, and the power of his Christ: for the accuser of our brethren is cast down, which accused them before our God day and night.

11 And **they** [the righteous premortal spirits] **overcame him** [Satan and his evil teachings and ways] **by the blood of the Lamb** [the Atonement of Christ], and by the word of their testimony; and they [righteous mortals] loved not their lives unto the death.

Jeffrey R. Holland

"We could remember that even in the Grand Council of Heaven [in the premortal realm] he loved us and was wonderfully strong, **that we triumphed even there by the power of Christ and our faith in the blood of the Lamb**" ("'This Do in Remembrance of Me,'" *Ensign,* November 1995, 68).

Q: Does that mean we could sin and repent in our pre-mortal life?

A: Yes.

New Testament Student Manual

"We were given laws and agency, and commandments to have faith and **repent from the wrongs that we could do there**" (in our premortal life) (*The Life and Teachings of Jesus and His Apostles: New Testament Student Manual*, 336).

"**Man could and did in many instances, sin before he was born**" (Joseph Fielding Smith, *The Way to Perfection*, 44; see also *The Life and Teachings of Jesus and His Apostles: New Testament Student Manual*, 336).

Q: Did the Atonement open the way for us to progress in our premortal life, as it does for us in mortality?

A: Yes.

As we learn more of the doctrines of the Plan of Salvation, it is important for us to understand that we, as spirit children of God before we came to earth, had been taught the gospel of Christ and given agency. Therefore, we could make choices. With this knowledge and agency, we could make mistakes and we could repent. We could also, therefore, make progress. The Atonement of Christ, as mentioned in the quotes above, worked for us there and enabled us to make progress, just as it does here on earth. This is no doubt how some spirits progressed to the point of being counted among "the noble and great ones" (Abraham 3:22). In other words, in many significant ways, our education toward exaltation during our premortal probationary period was similar to our probationary period here on earth. We have been well prepared for this mortal existence by the things we learned in our pre-earth life.

Some may wonder how the Atonement could work for us before it was actually accomplished here on earth. The answers to two simple questions that follow will explain how that is possible.

Q: Did the Savior's Atonement work before it was accomplished by Him here on earth? In other words, did it work for Alma and others who lived before the time of Christ's mortal mission and atoning sacrifice?

A: Yes.

Even though we cannot comprehend it completely, the Atonement of Jesus Christ is infinite. In other words, it goes in all directions. Thus, it not only worked for Alma, Amulek, Zeezrom, Adam and Eve, Lehi and Sariah, and others who lived on earth before the Savior's mortal ministry, but it also worked for all who chose to use it in the premortal realm before it was even accomplished. There was no resurrection on earth until Jesus came forth from the tomb, but there was forgiveness of sin.

Q: Is it true that Jesus was the firstborn spirit child of Heavenly Father?

A: Yes

The reason we often refer to Jesus as our "Elder Brother" is that He is, indeed, the oldest spirit child of our Heavenly Father and, thus, is our oldest spirit brother. The following quotes teach this clearly:

Colossians 1:13–15
13 Who [the Father] hath delivered us from the power of darkness, and hath translated us into the kingdom of **his dear Son** [Jesus Christ]:

14 In whom we have redemption through his blood, even the forgiveness of sins:

15 Who is the image of the invisible God [he looks just like the Father, who cannot be seen except under special circumstances], the **firstborn of every creature.**

D&C 93:21

21 And now, verily I say unto you, **I was in the beginning with the Father, and am the Firstborn.**

President Joseph F. Smith

"**Among the spirit children of Elohim** [Heavenly Father], **the first-born was and is Jehovah, or Jesus Christ,** to whom all others are juniors" (*Gospel Doctrine,* 70; see *also Doctrines of the Gospel Student Manual,* 9).

President Heber J. Grant

"We believe absolutely that Jesus Christ is the Son of God, begotten of God, **the first-born in the spirit** and the Only Begotten in the flesh" ("Analysis of the Articles of Faith," *Millennial Star,* 5 January 1922, 2; see also *Doctrines of the Gospel Student Manual,* 9).

Q: Why has the devil tried so hard to take away any belief in the concept that we existed before this earth life or that we will live beyond the grave?

A: He wants to destroy any and all sense of real purpose and worth in our lives.

As mentioned previously, perhaps you have noticed that one of Satan's basic approaches to tempting and destroying is to reduce human life to having no value at all. One way he does this is through promoting the false doctrine that we began life as mortals and that life ceases when we die. This doctrine boils down to the notion that we are a biological accident careening through space on a planet that accidentally brought forth life that has no ultimate purpose. When Satan succeeds in persuading us to believe this, he takes away all real purpose, all sense of permanence, and all feelings of inherent individual worth, and he ultimately destroys belief in God and the accountability that goes with it.

Korihor taught this basic, devilish doctrine with the following results:

Alma 30:17–18

17 And many more such things did he [Korihor] say unto them, telling them that there could be **no atonement** made for the sins of men, but **every man fared in this life according to the management of the creature** [we are on our own]; therefore every man prospered according to his genius, and that every man conquered according to his strength; and **whatsoever a man did was no crime.** [There is no such thing as right and wrong, good and evil, sin and righteousness.]

18 And thus he did preach unto them, leading away the hearts of many, **causing them to lift up their heads** [to become prideful] **in their wickedness,** yea, leading away many women, and also men, **to commit whoredoms** [sexual immorality]—telling them **that when a man was dead, that was the end thereof** [there is no life after death, no accountability, no Judgment Day, no real purpose in life; therefore, do whatever you want].

The fact is that we have existed forever. It is also a fact that we cannot cease to exist. No matter what we do on earth, when we die our spirit continues living. Everyone who has ever been born will be resurrected and will continue living throughout eternity as intelligence, spirit body, and physical body, inseparably joined together. The Book of Mormon teaches that if we were not to be resurrected because of the Atonement of Christ, we would all become devils.

2 Nephi 9:8–9

8 O the wisdom of God, his mercy and grace! For behold, **if the flesh should rise no more** [if we were not resurrected] our spirits must become subject to that angel [Lucifer] who fell from before the presence of the Eternal God, and became the devil, to rise no more.

9 And **our spirits must have** [would have] **become like unto him, and we become devils, angels to a devil,** to be shut out from the presence of our God, and **to remain with the father of lies** [Satan], in misery, like unto himself; yea, to that being who beguiled our first parents, who transformeth himself nigh unto an angel of light, and stirreth up the children of men unto secret combinations of murder and all manner of secret works of darkness.

Knowing that we are unavoidably eternal beings is one of the most important foundational doctrines of the Plan of Salvation.

The Council in Heaven

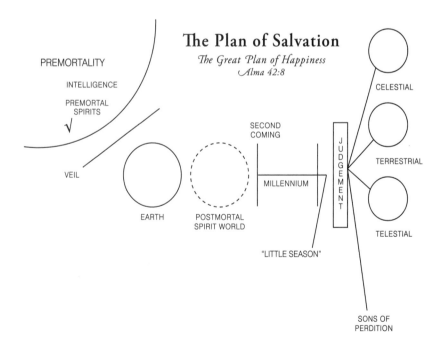

After living with our Heavenly Parents for eons as spirit children, we had progressed to the point that it was time to create an earth for us and give us the opportunity to come to it through the process of mortal birth. At this point, a Grand Council was called in heaven, which we all attended. The plan to create this earth was presented and explained to us, and we were given the opportunity to use our agency to accept it or reject it. We were overjoyed at the prospects of coming to earth, and we "shouted for joy," as described in Job:

Job 38:4, 7

4 Where wast thou when I laid the foundations of the earth?

7 When **the morning stars sang together, and all the sons of God** [spirit sons and daughters of God] **shouted for joy?**

The Prophet Joseph Smith taught that we all attended this premortal council in heaven and saw the Savior chosen as our Redeemer.

Joseph Smith

"At the first organization in heaven we were all present, and saw the Savior chosen and appointed and the plan of salvation made, and we sanctioned [approved] it" (*Teachings of the Prophet Joseph Smith*, 181).

Q: Was the Grand Council in Heaven for all of Father's children or just our group—those who were assigned to this earth?

A: Good question.

When you stop to think about it, our Heavenly Parents are still having spirit children. They are still clothing intelligence or intelligences with spirit bodies and teaching and preparing them to someday be sent to an earth to experience the same stages of progression through which we are passing. They will continue to have spirit children forever. This is one of the definitions of exaltation. The phrase "eternal lives" (D&C 132:24) is another term for exaltation. Thus, it would be logical to conclude that there are councils in heaven, as needed, for each group that is ready to be sent to an earth. Our council was held when our group was ready. A quote from President Joseph Fielding Smith helps us understand this:

Joseph Fielding Smith

"The beginning was when the councils met and the decision was made to create this earth that **the spirits who were intended for this earth,** should come here and partake of the mortal conditions and receive bodies of flesh and bones" (*Church History and Modern Revelation,* 1:401).

In 1916, the First Presidency explained that those of us who become gods would use the same Plan of Salvation for our spirit children as was used for us as we progressed toward exaltation ourselves. In other words, we will send our spirit children through the same steps of progression and give them the same opportunities for progression that we were given, including premortal spirit birth, the gospel, mortality on an earth, the spirit world, the Millennium, final judgment, and so forth. Thus, it appears that if we become gods, we will convene premortal councils for our own spirit offspring as needed.

The First Presidency

"Only resurrected and glorified [exalted] beings can become parents of spirit offspring. Only such exalted souls have reached maturity in the appointed course of eternal life; and **the spirits born to them in the eternal worlds will pass in due sequence through the several stages or estates by which the glorified parents have attained exaltation**" ("1916 First Presidency Statement," *Improvement Era,* August 1916, 942).

Q: Is there a fixed number of Heavenly Father's spirit children who are assigned to come to this earth?

A: Yes.

Elder James E. Talmage taught the following:

James E. Talmage
"The population of the earth is fixed according to the number of spirits appointed to take tabernacles of flesh upon this planet; when these have all come forth in the order and time appointed, then, and not till then, shall the end come" (*Articles of Faith*, 192–94).

Q: What do the terms "first estate" and "second estate" mean as used in gospel discussions about the Plan of Salvation?

A: "First estate" refers to our premortal life. "Second estate" refers to our mortal life.

The book of Abraham contains the most often-quoted scriptural passage using these two terms:

Abraham 3:25–26
25 And we will prove them herewith, to see if they will do all things whatsoever the Lord their God shall command them;

26 And they who **keep their first estate** [prove worthy, in premortality, to be sent to earth] shall be added upon [will be sent to earth]; and they who keep not their first estate shall not have glory in the same kingdom with those who keep their first estate; and they who **keep their second estate** [pass the tests of mortality] shall have glory added upon their heads for ever and ever [will be given exaltation].

These two terms are important to understand. As noted above, "first estate" refers to our premortal life. It includes the learning, progression, and testing that we underwent there and the choices we made. "Second estate" refers to our mortal life and testing, and includes the work going on in the spirit world for those who receive the gospel there. Those who kept their "first estate" (Abraham 3:26) earned the privilege of coming to earth to receive a physical body and continue progressing. Those who did not "keep their first estate" were the one-third who were cast out with Satan. Those who "keep their second estate" qualify for exaltation because they are faithful and pass the test here on earth (or in the spirit world).

The War in Heaven

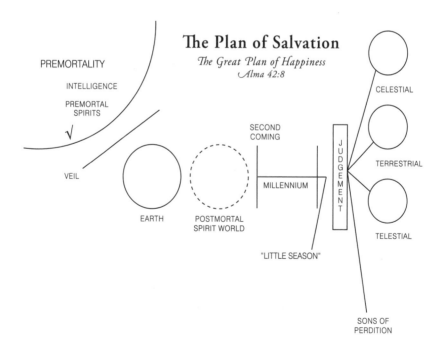

The Plan of Salvation
The Great Plan of Happiness
Alma 42:8

PREMORTALITY

INTELLIGENCE

PREMORTAL SPIRITS

√

VEIL

EARTH

POSTMORTAL SPIRIT WORLD

SECOND COMING

MILLENNIUM

"LITTLE SEASON"

JUDGEMENT

CELESTIAL

TERRESTRIAL

TELESTIAL

SONS OF PERDITION

The War in Heaven was a war in which we all participated, to one degree or another. The book of Revelation speaks of it as follows:

Revelation 12:7

7 And there was **war in heaven:** Michael [Adam] and his angels fought against the dragon [Lucifer]; and the dragon fought and his angels [followers],

8 And prevailed not [did not win]; neither was their place found any more in heaven.

9 And the great dragon was cast out, that old serpent, called the Devil, and Satan, which deceiveth the whole world: he was cast out into the earth, and his angels were cast out with him.

This war is described in the Bible Dictionary, contained in the LDS version of the Bible:

"War in Heaven. This term arises out of Rev. 12:7 and refers to **the conflict that took place in the premortal existence among the spirit children of God.** The war was primarily over how and in what manner the plan of salvation would be administered to the forthcoming human family upon the earth. **The issues involved such things as agency, how to gain salvation, and who should be the Redeemer.** The war broke out because one-third of the spirits refused to accept the appointment of Jesus Christ as the Savior. Such a refusal was a rebellion against the Father's plan of redemption. It was evident that if given agency, some persons would fall short of complete salvation; Lucifer and his followers wanted salvation to come automatically to all who passed through mortality, without regard to individual preference, agency, or voluntary dedication (see Isa. 14:12–20; Luke 10:18; Rev. 12:4–13; D&C 29:36–38; Moses 4:1–4). **The spirits who thus rebelled and persisted were thrust out of heaven and cast down to the earth without mortal bodies,** 'and thus came the devil and his angels' (D&C 29:37; see also Rev. 12:9; Abr. 3:24–28).

"The warfare is continued in mortality in the conflict between right and wrong, between the gospel and false principles, etc. The same contestants and the same issues are doing battle, and the same salvation is at stake.

"Although one-third of the spirits became devils, the remaining two-thirds were not all equally valiant, there being every degree of devotion to Christ and the Father among them. The most diligent were chosen to be rulers in the kingdom (Abr. 3:22–23). The nature of the conflict, however, is such that there could be no neutrals, then or now (Matt. 12:30; 1 Ne. 14:10; Alma 5:38–40)."

We will ask a few questions now about the War in Heaven by way of review.

Q: What kind of a war was it?

A: A battle over our moral agency and for our souls and our loyalty.

Spirits cannot be killed or destroyed such that they cease to exist. Therefore, this war would have been a war of words, ideas, and truth vs. falsehood, philosophies, etc. It was a battle for our loyalty, our minds, and our moral agency. President Gordon B. Hinckley spoke of this during the concluding session of general conference on April 6, 2003. In reference to the War in Heaven, he said:

Gordon B. Hinckley
"The book of Revelation speaks briefly of what must have been a terrible conflict for the **minds and loyalties** of God's children" ("War and Peace," *Ensign*, May 2003, 78). He then quoted Revelation 12:7–9.

Q: Was the War in Heaven concluded at that time?
A: No. It is continuing here on earth.

The war in heaven was not concluded there but is continuing here on earth, as Satan and his evil spirits, as well as his wicked mortal followers, continue to attempt to strip us of our agency and persuade us to follow them. The quote above from the Bible Dictionary indicates this. President Gordon B. Hinckley taught this doctrine during general conference in April 1995:

> **Gordon B. Hinckley**
> "Of course, there are some who do not measure up. That has been the case since the time of the great **War in Heaven** described by John the Revelator. **The issue then was free agency as it is today.** Then, as now, choices had to be made.
>
> "And there was war in heaven: Michael and his angels fought against the dragon; and the dragon fought and his angels,
>
> "And prevailed not; neither was their place found any more in heaven.
>
> "And the great dragon was cast out, that old serpent, called the Devil, and Satan, which deceiveth the whole world: he was cast out into the earth, and his angels were cast out with him (Rev. 12:7–9).
>
> **"That ancient struggle continues,** the unrelenting battle that comes of free agency" ("We Have a Work to Do," *Ensign,* May 1995, 87).

Thus, this battle for our souls will continue until it is concluded at the end of the Battle of Gog and Magog, after the Millennium. This final battle is described briefly in the Doctrine and Covenants:

D&C 88:111–15

111 And then he shall be loosed for a little season, that he may gather together his armies.

112 And Michael, the seventh angel, even the archangel, shall gather together his armies, even the hosts of heaven.

113 And the devil shall gather together his armies; even the hosts of hell, and shall come up to battle against Michael and his armies.

114 And then cometh the battle of the great God [the battle of Gog and Magog; see Bible Dictionary, "Gog"]; and **the devil and his armies shall be cast away into their own place, that they shall not have power over the saints any more at all.**

115 For Michael shall fight their battles, and shall overcome him who seeketh the throne of him who sitteth upon the throne, even the Lamb.

Q: Where did Satan and the spirits who followed him go?

A: They were cast down to earth.

Revelation 12:4

"And his tail drew the third part of the stars of heaven, and did **cast them to the earth.**"

Q: Were there any "neutrals" in the War in Heaven? In other words, were there any who did not eventually take sides, using their individual agency to decide?

A: No.

Some people believe the mistaken notion that there were some fence-sitters during the War in Heaven. This is not the case.

Joseph Fielding Smith addressed this issue:

Joseph Fielding Smith

"There were no neutrals in the war in heaven. *All took sides either with Christ or with Satan.* Every man had his agency there, and men receive rewards here based upon their actions there, just as they will receive rewards hereafter for deeds done in the body" (*Doctrines of Salvation,* 1:65–66).

CHAPTER THREE

THE CREATION

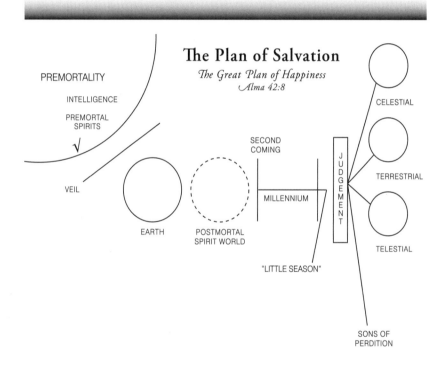

The Plan of Salvation
The Great Plan of Happiness
Alma 42:8

PREMORTALITY

INTELLIGENCE

PREMORTAL
SPIRITS

VEIL

EARTH

POSTMORTAL
SPIRIT WORLD

SECOND
COMING

MILLENNIUM

"LITTLE SEASON"

JUDGEMENT

CELESTIAL

TERRESTRIAL

TELESTIAL

SONS OF
PERDITION

Whe the appropriate time arrived, the earth was created for us. It was created by the Savior, under the direction of the Father. Moses teaches this clearly, as follows:

Moses 1:32–33

32 And by the word of my power [through Christ], have I [the Father] created them [this world, as well as countless others], which is mine Only Begotten Son, who is full of grace and truth.

33 And worlds without number have I created; and I also created them for mine own purpose; and **by the Son I created them,** which is mine Only Begotten.

Interesting questions abound as to how the earth was created, how long it took, where dinosaurs fit in, and so forth. But the important fact is that it was created as a part of the Plan of Salvation for us and that it was not a chance happening. We will continue by posing a number of commonly asked questions.

Q: How long did it take to create the earth?
A: We don't know.

The most common answer to this question is that the Creation took six thousand years. This is based on the belief that each of the six days of creation lasted a thousand years. This belief probably comes from combining the fact that "one day is with the Lord as a thousand years" (2 Peter 3:8) with an assumption that each "day" of creation as described in Genesis 1 and Moses 2 lasted one thousand years. We need to be cautious about interpreting the above references so absolutely.

Abraham was a great astronomer as well as a prophet (see Abraham 3). He used the term "time" (see Abraham 4:8, 13, 19, etc.), which leaves open the duration of each "day" of the Creation. We will examine some of these verses from Abraham, using **bold** for emphasis in the scriptures and other citations.

Abraham 4:8, 13, 19, 23, 31

8 And the Gods called the expanse, Heaven. And it came to pass that it was from evening until morning that they called night; and it came to pass that it was from morning until evening that they called day; and this was **the second time** that they called night and day.

13 And it came to pass that they numbered the days; from the evening until the morning they called night; and it came to pass, from the morning until the evening they called day; and it was **the third time.**

19 And it came to pass that it was from evening until morning that it was night; and it came to pass that it was from morning until evening that it was day; and it was **the fourth time.**

23 And it came to pass that it was from evening until morning that they called night; and it came to pass that it was from morning until evening that they called day; and it was **the fifth time.**

31 And the Gods said: We will do everything that we have said, and organize them; and behold, they shall be very obedient. And it came to pass that it was from evening until morning they called night; and it came to pass that it was from morning until evening that they called day; and they numbered **the sixth time.**

The *Doctrines of the Gospel Student Manual,* 2000 edition, quotes Elder Bruce R. McConkie on this subject:

Bruce R. McConkie
"But first, what is a day? It is a specified time period; it is an age, an eon, a division of eternity; it is the time between two identifiable events. And each day, of whatever length, has the duration needed for its purposes. . . . **There is no revealed recitation specifying that each of the 'six days' involved in the creation was of the same duration**" (*Doctrines of the Gospel Student Manual,* 17).

Q: Will we eventually receive more information and detail about how the earth was created, how long it took, and so forth?

A: Yes.

It is important that we do not get caught up in arguments as to how long it took to create the earth. We do know for sure that the Lord created it. In fact, if you read Genesis 1 carefully, you will see more than forty ways in which the Lord says, in effect, "I created the earth." Another important thing to know is that Jesus will give us more details about the creation of the earth when He comes again, as stated in the Doctrine and Covenants:

D&C 101:32–34

32 Yea, verily I say unto you, in that day **when the Lord shall come, he shall reveal all things—**

33 Things which have passed, and hidden things which no man knew, **things of the earth, by which it was made,** and the purpose and the end thereof—

34 Things most precious, things that are above, and things that are beneath, things that are in the earth, and upon the earth, and in heaven.

Q: Did others help create the earth?

A: Yes.

In the book of Abraham, the Savior invites the "noble and great ones" to help Him create the earth:

Abraham 3:22–24

22 Now the Lord had shown unto me, Abraham, the intelligences [spirits; see v. 23] that were organized before the world was; and **among all these there were many of the noble and great ones;**

23 And God saw these souls [spirits] that they were

good, and he stood in the midst of them, and he said: These I will make my rulers; for he stood among those that were spirits, and he saw that they were good; and he said unto me: Abraham, thou art one of them; thou wast chosen before thou wast born.

24 And there stood one among them that was like unto God [the premortal Christ], and he said unto those who were with him: We will go down, for there is space there, and we will take of these materials, and we will make an earth whereon these [all of the spirits assigned to this earth] may dwell.

Others have taught the same thing, including Joseph Fielding Smith:

Joseph Fielding Smith

"It is true that **Adam helped to form this earth.** He labored with our Savior Jesus Christ. **I have a strong view or conviction that there were others also who assisted them.** Perhaps Noah and Enoch; and *why not Joseph Smith*, and those who were appointed to be rulers before the earth was formed?" (*Doctrines of Salvation*, 1:74–75).

Q: Did we evolve from lower forms of life?

A: No, according to the First Presidency.

The First Presidency—Joseph F. Smith, John R. Winder, and Anthon H. Lund

"It is held by some that Adam was not the first man upon this earth, and that the original human being was a development from lower orders of the animal creation. These, however, are the theories of men. The word of the Lord declares that Adam was 'the first man of all men' (Moses 1:34), and we are therefore in duty bound to regard him as the primal parent of our race. It was shown to the

brother of Jared that all men were created in the beginning after the image of God; and whether we take this to
mean the spirit or the body, or both, it commits us to the
same conclusion: **Man began life as a human being, in
the likeness of our heavenly Father**" (*Improvement Era*,
1909, 13:75–61; see also Clark, *Messages of the First Presidency*, 4:205; *Doctrines of the Gospel Student Manual*, 17).

From the same First Presidency statement, we read:

The First Presidency
"**All men and women are in the similitude of the
Universal Father and Mother** and are literally the sons
and daughters of deity. . . . 'God created man in his own
image.' This is just as true of the spirit as it is of the body,
which is only the clothing of the spirit, its complement;
the two together constituting the soul. The spirit of man
is in the form of man, and the spirits of all creations are
in the likeness of their bodies. This was plainly taught by
the Prophet Joseph Smith (D&C 77:2)" (Clark, *Messages
of the First Presidency*, 4:203).

Q: Was Eve taken from one of Adam's ribs?
A: No.

President Spencer W. Kimball taught that the account of the
"rib," as given in the scriptures (Genesis 2:21–24; Moses 3:21–23;
Abraham 5:15–17), is symbolic rather than literal:

Spencer W. Kimball
"And I, God, created man in mine own image, in the
image of mine Only Begotten created I him; male and
female created I them. **[The story of the rib, of course,
is figurative.]**" ("The Blessings and Responsibilities of
Womanhood," *Ensign*, March 1976, 71–73).

Knowing that the account is symbolic opens the door to some beautiful imagery and meaning. For instance, Eve was "formed" from an area near Adam's heart, and so they walk side by side, not one ahead of or behind the other. She is protected by his arm (arm is symbolic of power in biblical culture), and they work together, side by side, in harmony and unity. (Eve is now "bone of my bones, and flesh of my flesh" [Genesis 2:24]). Their loyalty to each other is even greater than their loyalty to their parents. "Therefore shall a man leave his father and his mother, and shall cleave unto his wife" (Genesis 2:24), and they become "one flesh" (Genesis 2:24), symbolizing unity, harmony, enjoying being together as eternal companions, as well as bringing children into the world.

Q: Why do the scriptures make the story of the rib sound so literal if it is merely symbolic?

A: This is typical of biblical culture and writing.

We Westerners (residents of the Western hemisphere, especially of the United States and Canada) tend to want things to be literal, and much of our writing and culture reflects this. However, such is not the case with many other cultures, including biblical and other Eastern cultures. Thus, much of their writing is highly symbolic, transferring emotion and feeling, as well as fact, to the reader.

So it is that the scriptural accounts of the creation of Eve give much more than the fact that she came on the scene. They provide drama and feeling, warmth and tenderness, belonging and protectiveness, unity and purpose to the account, far beyond the fact of Adam and Eve's coming forth to fulfill their role in "the great plan of happiness" (Alma 42:8).

Q: Was the earth created in its present location in the solar system?

A: No.

We understand from the teachings of President Brigham Young that the earth was created near where our Heavenly Father resides, and that it was moved to its particular area of space in this solar system at the time of the fall of Adam and Eve. We will quote Brigham Young and Joseph Smith on this subject:

Brigham Young

"This earth is our home, it was framed expressly for the habitation of those who are faithful to God, and who prove themselves worthy to inherit the earth when the Lord shall have sanctified, purified and glorified it and **brought it back into his presence, from which it fell far into space. . . . When the earth was framed and brought into existence and man was placed upon it, it was near the throne of our Father in heaven.** And when man fell . . . **the earth fell into space, and took up its abode in this planetary system,** and the sun became our light. . . . This is the glory the earth came from, and when it is **glorified it will return again unto the presence of the Father,** and it will dwell there, and these intelligent beings that I am looking at, if they live worthy of it, will dwell upon this earth" (in *Journal of Discourses*, 17:143).

Joseph Smith

"This earth will be **rolled back into the presence of God,** and crowned with celestial glory" (*Teachings of the Prophet Joseph Smith*, 181).

CHAPTER FOUR

THE FALL OF
ADAM AND EVE

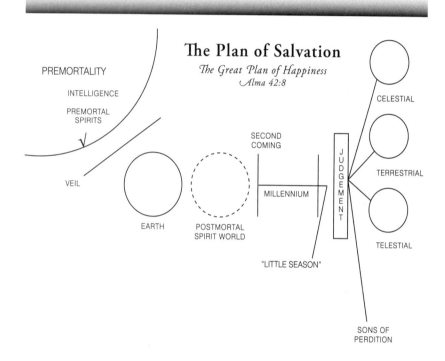

The Plan of Salvation

The Great Plan of Happiness
Alma 42:8

PREMORTALITY

INTELLIGENCE

PREMORTAL
SPIRITS

VEIL

EARTH

POSTMORTAL
SPIRIT WORLD

SECOND
COMING

MILLENNIUM

"LITTLE SEASON"

JUDGEMENT

CELESTIAL

TERRESTRIAL

TELESTIAL

SONS OF
PERDITION

We read about the fall of Adam and Eve in Genesis 3 and Moses 4, and it is referred to in numerous other scriptural passages. The Fall is an essential part of the Plan of Salvation. We will study Moses 4:20–25 in considerable detail in a few minutes, but we will take a quick look at several aspects of the Fall before we do.

Q: Was the Fall good or bad?
A: Good!

First and foremost, the Fall was good and absolutely essential for our continued progress. Without it, we could not have come to earth. In our gospel discussions, we sometimes say that Adam and Eve "fell forward," rather than "fell down." The fact that the Fall was good is emphasized in a number of scriptural passages. We will quote two here, using **bold** for teaching emphasis in these passages and in subsequent citations:

> **2 Nephi 2:22–25**
>
> 22 And now, behold, **if Adam had not transgressed he would not have fallen,** but he would have remained in the garden of Eden. **And all things** which were created **must have** [would have] **remained in the same state** in which they were after they were created; and they must have remained **forever,** and had no end.
>
> 23 And they would have had no children; wherefore they would have remained in a state of innocence, having **no joy,** for they knew **no misery;** doing **no good,** for they knew no sin.
>
> 24 But behold, **all things have been done in the wisdom of him who knoweth all things** [in other words, this was part of God's plan for us].
>
> 25 **Adam fell that men might be; and men are, that they might have joy.**

Moses 5:10–11

10 And in that day **Adam** blessed God and was filled, and began to prophesy concerning all the families of the earth, saying: Blessed be the name of God, for **because of my transgression my eyes are opened, and in this life I shall have joy,** and again in the flesh I shall see God.

11 And **Eve,** his wife, heard all these things and **was glad,** saying: Were it not for our transgression we never should have had seed [children], and never should have known good and evil, and the joy of our redemption, and the eternal life which God giveth unto all the obedient.

Q: Was the Fall unexpected? In other words, was heaven caught off guard by it?

A: No.

In fact, it was planned by God and happened just as He planned. President Brigham Young makes this clear:

Brigham Young

"Did they [Adam and Eve] come out in direct opposition to God and to his government? No. But they transgressed a command of the Lord, and through that transgression sin came into the world. **The Lord knew they would do this, and he had designed** [planned] **that they should**" (*Discourses of Brigham Young,* 103; see also *Doctrines of the Gospel Student Manual,* 21).

As Latter-day Saints, we stand virtually alone among all Christian churches in teaching that the Fall was good. Almost all others teach that it was a bad mistake and brought nothing but sin and suffering into the world. As a result, many look upon Adam and Eve with resentment and criticism. In fact, many abuses of women have been blamed upon Eve because of misperceptions about her vital role in this step forward for all of us. We will say more about her role in the Fall in a minute.

Q: What about the two "conflicting" commandments, in which Adam and Eve are told to have children but not to eat the fruit of the tree (Genesis 1:28; 2:17)?

A: There appears to be more to the story.

Joseph Fielding Smith

"Now this is the way I interpret that: The Lord said to Adam, here is the Tree of the Knowledge of Good and Evil. If you want to stay here, then you cannot eat of that fruit. If you want to stay here, then I forbid you to eat it. But you may act for yourself, and you may eat of it if you want to. And if you eat it, you will die" (*Charge to Religious Educators,* page 124; see also *Doctrines of the Gospel Student Manual,* 20).

Quoting further from Joseph Fielding Smith:

Joseph Fielding Smith:

"Just why the Lord would say to Adam that he forbade him to partake of the fruit of that tree is not made clear in the Bible account, but in the original as it comes to us in the book of Moses it is made definitely clear. It is that the Lord said to Adam that **if he wished to remain** as he was in the garden, then he was not to eat the fruit, **but if he desired to eat it and partake of death** he was at liberty to do so. So really it was not in the true sense a transgression of a divine commandment. Adam made the wise decision, in fact the only decision that he could make.

"It was the divine plan from the very beginning that man should be placed on the earth and be subject to mortal conditions and pass through a probationary state" (*Answers to Gospel Questions,* 4:81).

Q: Adam and Eve were innocent in the Garden of Eden, but does that mean that they had no knowledge at all with which to make decisions?

A: No.

Elder John A. Widtsoe

"Such was the problem before our first parents: to remain forever at selfish ease in the Garden of Eden, or to face unselfishly tribulation and death, in bringing to pass the purposes of the Lord for a host of waiting spirit children. They chose the latter. . . . **This they did with open eyes and minds as to consequences.** The memory of their former estates [including their premortal spirit existence] may have been dimmed, **but the gospel had been taught them during their sojourn in the Garden of Eden.** . . . the choice that they made raises Adam and Even to pre-eminence among all who have come on earth" (*Evidences and Reconciliations*, 193–94).

Elder George Albert Smith:

"When God created the earth and placed our first parents upon it, **He did not leave them without knowledge concerning Himself.** It is true that there had been taken from them the remembrance of their pre-existent life, but in His tender mercy He talked with them and later He sent His choice servants to instruct them in the things pertaining to eternal life (in Conference Report, October 1928, 90–91).

Q: Was Eve completely fooled by Satan's temptation in the Garden?

A: No. She made a deliberate, informed decision to partake of the fruit.

The *Encyclopedia of Mormonism*

"Satan was present to tempt Adam and Eve, much as he would try to thwart others in their divine missions: 'and he sought also to beguile Eve, for he knew not the mind of God, wherefore he sought to destroy the world' (Moses 4:6). **Eve faced the choice between selfish ease and unselfishly facing tribulation and death** (John A. Widtsoe, *Evidences and Reconciliations*, 193). As befit her calling, she realized that there was no other way and **deliberately chose mortal life so as to further the purpose of God and bring children into the world**" (see "Eve").

Q: Why does Paul say that Eve was deceived (1 Timothy 2:14)?

A: No doubt she was, in some ways.

We will probably have to wait until we get a chance to talk to Eve herself, perhaps during the Millennium, for the complete account. If you read carefully what she said in scriptural accounts, you will be reminded that she asked important and intelligent questions before partaking of the fruit, and she responded with unselfishness. Yet there could be many ways in which she was deceived. Perhaps in the sense of not believing that mortality would be so difficult at times. Perhaps she had no idea what it would be like to care for twenty or thirty sick children when they all had the flu! Maybe she was deceived into thinking that old age, with its attendant pains and disabilities, would not be that difficult. Actually, she couldn't have understood these physical struggles because she had no basis on which to judge. She and her husband were not yet mortal, even though they had physical bodies at this point.

Q: How many lies did the devil use in the recorded tempting of Adam and Eve?

A: Just one.

We will take a quick look at the temptation scene in the Garden of Eden, using Genesis 3 as our main reference. We will see that the devil mixed a lie with some truths—an approach he often uses in tempting us today.

Genesis 3:4–5

4 And the serpent said unto the woman, **Ye shall not surely die** [the lie]:

5 For God doth know that in the day ye eat thereof, **then your eyes shall be opened** [true], **and ye shall be as gods, knowing good and evil** [true].

Q: Was Adam and Eve's partaking of the fruit a sin (Genesis 3:6; Moses 4:12)?

A: No. It was what God wanted them to do.

Joseph Fielding Smith

"What did Adam do? The very thing the Lord wanted him to do; and I hate to hear anybody call it a sin, for **it wasn't a sin**. . . . I see a great difference between transgressing the law and committing a sin" (*Charge to Religious Educators*, 124; see *also Doctrines of the Gospel Student Manual*, 20).

Q: If it wasn't a sin, then why did the Lord "curse" them for doing it (Genesis 3:13–19; Moses 4:20–23)?

A: He didn't.

He didn't curse Adam and Eve. Read Genesis 3:13–19 more

carefully. He cursed two things: the serpent (v. 14) and the ground (v. 17). In fact, the ground was cursed "for thy sake." In other words, it was a blessing for Adam and Eve (see also Moses 4:20–23). Joseph Fielding Smith explained this follows.

Joseph Fielding Smith

"When Adam was driven out of the Garden of Eden, the Lord passed a sentence upon him. Some people have looked upon that sentence as being a dreadful thing. It was not; **it was a blessing. . . .** In order for mankind to obtain salvation and exaltation it is necessary for them to obtain bodies in this world, and pass through the experiences and schooling that are found only in mortality. . . . The fall of man came as a blessing in disguise, and was the means of furthering the purposes of the Lord in the progress of man, rather than a means of hindering them" (*Doctrines of Salvation,* 1:113–14; see *also Doctrines of the Gospel Student Manual,* 21).

Q: If it wasn't a curse, why do the scriptures make it look like it was?

A: Read the scriptures more carefully, especially Genesis 3:15–17, Moses 4:20–23, and 2 Nephi 2:22–27, and you will see this from a different perspective.

The accounts in Genesis and Moses must be read in the light of other scriptures and in the overall teachings of the Plan of Salvation. The words of modern prophets and apostles must also be studied. Many people, including members of the Church, have not done this, and thus, much misinformation and false doctrine continue to be taught on this topic.

We will take a few moments here to study these passages of scripture, adding lengthy notes in brackets and using **bold** for emphasis. We will use the account given in the book of Moses.

Moses 4:20–25

20 And I, the Lord God, said unto **the serpent** [Lucifer; see heading to Genesis 3 in the LDS Bible]: Because thou hast done this **thou shalt be cursed** above all cattle, and above every beast of the field [they all get physical bodies, but Lucifer doesn't; Joseph Smith taught, "The devil has no body, and herein is his punishment" *(Teachings of the Prophet Joseph Smith*, 181)]; upon thy belly shalt thou go, and dust shalt thou eat all the days of thy life; [one simple way to look at this last phrase is to say that the devil will always be behind the Savior, in effect, eating His dust].

21 And I will put enmity [a natural dislike, abhorrence, squeamishness] between thee and the woman, between thy seed [Satan's followers] and her seed ["The seed of the woman refers to Jesus Christ" (*Old Testament Student Manual*, 41; see also James E. Talmage, *Jesus the Christ*, 43)]; and he [Christ] shall bruise [crush; defeat] thy head [Christ will have ultimate victory over Satan and his kingdom], and thou [Lucifer] shalt bruise his [Christ's] heel [Lucifer will cause trouble for Christ and His faithful followers, including inciting evil people to crucify Christ; the imagery is of a snake biting a man's heel, being thus dragged along, inflicting pain, but not stopping him].

22 Unto the woman [Eve], I, the Lord God, said: **I will greatly multiply thy sorrow and thy conception** [because of Eve's choice in the Garden of Eden, she will now be able to have many children]. **In sorrow** [the same Hebrew word is used for Adam's situation in verse 23, implying mortality and its associated cares, travail, pain, etc., rather than punishment; President Spencer W. Kimball said, "I wonder if those who translated the Bible might have used the term *distress* instead of sorrow. It would mean much the same, except I think there is great gladness in most Latter-day Saint homes when there is to be a child there" ("The Blessings and Responsibilities of Womanhood,"

Ensign, March 1976, 72)] **thou shalt bring forth children** [a happy thing], and thy desire [loyalty] shall be to thy husband, and he shall rule [preside in love and service, much the same as the Savior does; President Kimball preferred the word "preside" rather than "rule;" see same article quoted above] over thee.

23 And unto Adam, I, the Lord God, said: Because thou hast hearkened unto the voice of thy wife [which was a wise and unselfish thing for Adam to do], and hast eaten of the fruit of the tree of which I commanded thee, saying—Thou shalt not eat of it, cursed shall be the ground **for thy sake** [in other words, this will become a great benefit to you]; **in sorrow** [in a mortal world, with its accompanying pain, work, travail, and difficulties] shalt thou eat of it all the days of thy life.

24 Thorns also, and thistles shall it bring forth to thee, and thou shalt eat the herb of the field.

25 **By the sweat of thy face** shalt thou eat bread, until thou shalt return unto the ground—for thou shalt surely die—for out of it wast thou taken: for dust thou wast, and unto dust shalt thou return.

In summary, the fall of Adam and Eve, when viewed in the overall context of the Plan of Salvation, was very good and absolutely necessary. Obviously, it was a most serious step for Adam and Eve, and it took them into a much different world, such as when our sons and daughters depart for their missions. There are many tears and much sadness, even "sorrow"; nevertheless, there is great growth and satisfaction, as expressed by both Adam and Eve in Moses 5:10–11.

When we read the scriptural accounts of the Fall, we feel the seriousness of the occasion, and when we add other scriptures and doctrines taught by the Brethren, we sense the magnificence and greatness of our "first parents" as they intentionally took this marvelous step.

Q: Was there a Plan B in case Adam and Eve didn't partake of the fruit?

A: No.

As he teaches his son Jacob about the Fall in 2 Nephi 2, Lehi makes it clear that a Plan B was unnecessary. Both Joseph Fielding Smith and President Brigham Young taught this same doctrine.

2 Nephi 2:22–25

22 And now, behold, if Adam had not transgressed he would not have fallen, but he would have remained in the garden of Eden. And all things which were created must have remained in the same state in which they were after they were created; and they must have remained forever, and had no end.

23 And they would have had no children; wherefore they would have remained in a state of innocence, having no joy, for they knew no misery; doing no good, for they knew no sin.

24 But behold, **all things have been done in the wisdom of him who knoweth all things** [in other words, a Plan B was not needed].

25 Adam fell that men might be; and men are, that they might have joy.

Joseph Fielding Smith

"We came into this world to die. That was understood before we came here. It is part of the plan, all discussed and arranged long before men were placed upon the earth. **When Adam was sent into this world, it was with the understanding that he would violate a law, transgress a law, in order to bring to pass this mortal condition** which we find ourselves in today" (*Doctrines of Salvation*, 1:66; see also *Doctrines of the Gospel Student Manual*, 21).

Brigham Young

"Did they [Adam and Eve] come out in direct opposition to God and to his government? No. But they transgressed a command of the Lord, and through that transgression sin came into the world. **The Lord knew they would do this, and he had designed that they should**" (*Discourses of Brigham Young*, 103; see also *Doctrines of the Gospel Student Manual*, 21).

CHAPTER FIVE

THE ATONEMENT OF CHRIST

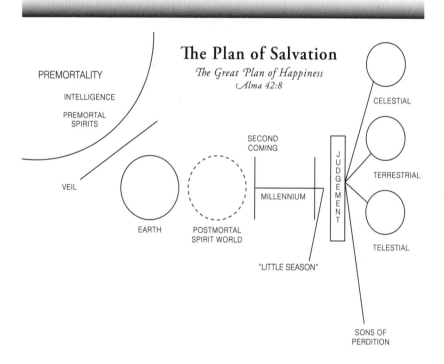

The Plan of Salvation
The Great Plan of Happiness
Alma 42:8

PREMORTALITY

INTELLIGENCE

PREMORTAL
SPIRITS

VEIL

EARTH

POSTMORTAL
SPIRIT WORLD

SECOND
COMING

MILLENNIUM

"LITTLE SEASON"

JUDGEMENT

CELESTIAL

TERRESTRIAL

TELESTIAL

SONS OF
PERDITION

The Atonement of Christ is central to everything we do. The fall of Adam and Eve and the Atonement go hand in hand. They are both integral and vital parts of the Plan of Salvation. Perhaps you noticed that the check mark ($\sqrt{}$) that normally appears on the Plan of Salvation chart at the beginning of each chapter to indicate where we are in the plan does not appear on the chart above. That is because the Atonement applies in so many different settings represented by the chart.

As previously explained, the Savior's Atonement worked for us in our premortal life. It obviously is available for us here on earth. It also is effective in the postmortal spirit world, including for those in the spirit world mission field who await the cleansing ordinance of baptism for the dead, as performed for them by worthy Saints here on earth. It will continue to be effective for many during the Millennium and will even help those who are judged worthy of exaltation on the day of final judgment as they continue their growth and development until they become gods.

Thus, the Atonement of Jesus Christ is the crowning and all-pervasive central focus of the Plan of Salvation. It enables us to be optimists and to look forward with bright hope and anticipation to succeeding in our personal quest for exaltation. The gift of forgiveness, upon proper repentance, is priceless. The gift of personal progress is exciting. And the suffering of the Savior to make both possible is humbling to each who accepts His infinite and merciful gift by following Him back to the Father.

It is crucial in our study of the Atonement that we understand the following definitions of several central elements related to it. We will intentionally keep things simple and brief as we consider the following doctrines related to the Atonement:

Physical death: The separation of the body and spirit at the time of mortal death.

Resurrection: The permanent reuniting of the spirit and body.

Spiritual death: Losing the privilege of returning to live in the presence of God forever.

Justice: The law of justice (an eternal law) requires that all sins be paid for, whether by Christ's Atonement or by individuals themselves.

Mercy: The law of mercy allows Christ's Atonement to pay for our sins and thus satisfy the requirements of the law of justice, if we repent. Thus, we can be made clean and free from sin, worthy to enter the presence of God and enabled to continue progressing until we become gods.

Jesus Christ was chosen in the premortal realm to be our Savior and Redeemer. Through His unique earthly parentage, being the Son of the Eternal Father and the offspring of a mortal woman, He was enabled and empowered to carry out the Atonement for us. No other mortal could perform such an atoning sacrifice. His Atonement is infinite, meaning that it applies to all inhabitants of the Father's worlds—past, present, and future—and is constantly blessing us in all aspects of our lives as we earnestly strive to keep the commandments.

Because of the fall of Adam and Eve, all of us will die. We are all subject to physical death. This is a great blessing, a vital step for us as we journey through the various stages of the Plan of Salvation toward exaltation. Because of the Atonement, everyone who has ever been born will be resurrected, regardless of how they live their lives. In other words, the most wicked mortals as well as the most righteous will all be resurrected through the power of the Savior's atoning sacrifice and Resurrection.

The one-third who were cast out with Satan (Revelation 12:4) will not be resurrected because they will not be born on earth and thus will not receive a mortal body. It may well be that resurrection is far more important than many realize, as shown by the following question and answer:

Q: What would happen to us if we were not resurrected?

A: We would all become devils, completely subject to Satan.

Jacob taught this doctrine in the Book of Mormon when he instructed his people about the Atonement (**bold** is added for emphasis):

2 Nephi 9:8–9

8 O the wisdom of God, his mercy and grace! For behold, **if the flesh should rise no more** [if we were not to be resurrected] our spirits must become [would become] subject to that angel [Lucifer] who fell from before the presence of the Eternal God, and became the devil, to rise no more.

9 And **our spirits must have become like unto him,** and **we become devils,** angels to a devil, to be shut out from the presence of our God, and to remain with the father of lies [Satan], in misery, like unto himself; yea, to that being who beguiled our first parents, who transformeth himself nigh unto an angel of light, and stirreth up the children of men unto secret combinations of murder and all manner of secret works of darkness.

Q: Will those who are "twinkled" (changed in the twinkling of an eye during the Millennium) actually die and then be resurrected?

A: Yes.

The answer to this question is given in the Doctrine and Covenants:

D&C 101:31

31 And **when he dies** he shall not sleep, that is to say in the earth [he won't be buried in a grave], but shall **be changed in the twinkling of an eye,** and shall be caught up, and his rest shall be glorious.

Q: Does the term "spiritual death" mean the death of the spirit? In other words, do spirits get destroyed and cease to exist?

A: No.

Spiritual death, as mentioned earlier, is the loss of the privilege of returning to the presence of the Father to live forever. Sometimes people confuse this term with the death of the spirit. Spirits cannot die. They cannot cease to exist. Thus, spiritual death does not mean the literal death of the spirit; rather, it means the pursuing of a course of unrepentant wickedness, such that one loses personal righteousness and is not cleansed by the Atonement of Christ. The Book of Mormon teaches this:

> **Alma 12:11, 32**
>
> 11 And **they that will harden their hearts,** to them is given the lesser portion of the **word until they know nothing concerning his mysteries** [the simple doctrines of the gospel]; and then they are taken captive by the devil, and led by his will down to destruction. Now this is what is meant by **the chains of hell.**
>
> 32 Therefore God gave unto them commandments, after having made known unto them the plan of redemption, that they should not do evil, the penalty thereof being a second death [spiritual death], which was an everlasting **death as to things pertaining unto righteousness;** for on such the plan of redemption could have no power, for the works of justice could not be destroyed, according to the supreme goodness of God.

Q: How can a person overcome spiritual death?

A: Through the Atonement of Christ.

The scriptures and the words of modern prophets and apostles are filled with the wonderful message that we can overcome sin and personal shortcomings through the Atonement. Christ can make us clean. He can enable us to continue progressing. He paid the price, and if we come unto Him, He can set us free.

Q: Must we have a basic understanding of the law of justice and the law of mercy in order to understand how the Atonement works in our lives?

A: Yes.

Many basic misunderstandings about how the Atonement works for us are cleared up by a fundamental knowledge and understanding of the laws of justice and mercy. These two laws provide the framework within which we work out our salvation or lose it. The issues of agency and personal accountability are central to this discussion about justice, mercy, and the Atonement.

Let's begin with God's laws. Simply put, the universe is governed by law—God's law (see D&C 88:36–45). Laws provide dependability and stability. Fundamental stability must be in place before people can successfully exercise agency. The laws of justice and mercy provide us with a completely reliable frame of reference within which to exercise our God-given agency. If we use our agency wisely, the results are sure. If we use it foolishly, the results are sure.

God has given us laws governing personal progress. They are usually referred to as commandments. The law of justice requires that whenever a commandment is broken, a penalty must be paid. This is crucial in preserving the stability spoken of above. The law of mercy allows the Savior to pay for our sins, thus satisfying the law of justice. If we accept the Savior's payment, we are in debt to Him. A payment from us is thus required to the Savior, rather than to the law of justice. The merciful payment He requires of us, which leads to forgiveness of sins and cleansing from unrighteousness, is repentance. Repenting and keeping the commandments is how we access the law of mercy. Have you noticed that every requirement placed upon us for being forgiven of sins insists that we engage in behaviors that are designed to make us happy and promote peace in our lives?

Q: Did the Savior's suffering for our sins take place in the Garden of Gethsemane as well as on the cross, or just in Gethsemane?

A: Both.

The following quote answers this question:

Bruce R. McConkie

"To this we add, if we interpret the holy word aright, that all of the anguish, all of the sorrow, and all of the suffering of Gethsemane recurred during the final three hours on the cross, the hours when darkness covered the land. Truly there was no sorrow like unto his sorrow, and no anguish and pain like unto that which bore in with such intensity upon him" (*The Mortal Messiah*, 4:232 note 22; see *also Doctrines of the Gospel Student Manual*, 25).

Q: Does the Savior's Atonement work for our inadequacies and shortcomings, as well as for our sins?

A: Yes.

Elder Neal A. Maxwell taught this doctrine:

Neal A. Maxwell

"In Alma 7:12, the only place in scriptures, to my knowledge, that it appears, there seems to have been yet another purpose of the Atonement, speaking again of the Savior and his suffering, 'And he will take upon him death, that he may loose the bands of death which bind his people; and he will take upon him their infirmities, that his bowels may be filled with mercy, according to his flesh, that he may know according to the flesh, how to succor his people according to their infirmities.' Have you ever thought that there was no way that Jesus could know the suffering which we undergo as a result of our stupidity and sin (because he was sinless) except he bear those sins of ours in what I call the awful arithmetic of the Atonement? And according to this prophet, Jesus now knows, according to the flesh, how to succor us and how to help us as a result of that suffering, which knowledge could have come in no other way" ("The Old Testament: Relevancy within Antiquity," *A Symposium on the Old Testament*, 17; see also *Doctrines of the Gospel Student Manual*, 24–25).

Q: Can we ever pay off the debt we owe the Savior?
A: No. (This is actually a wonderful thing!)

King Benjamin explains:

Mosiah 2:22–24

22 And behold, **all that he requires of you is to keep his commandments;** and he has promised you that if ye would keep his commandments ye should prosper in the land; and he never doth vary from that which he hath said; therefore, **if ye do keep his commandments he doth bless you and prosper you.**

23 And now, in the first place, he hath created you, and granted unto you your lives, for which ye are indebted unto him.

24 And secondly, he doth require that ye should do as he hath commanded you; for **which if ye do, he doth immediately bless you; and therefore he hath paid you. And ye are still indebted unto him, and are, and will be, forever and ever;** therefore, of what have ye to boast?

Q: How often can we be forgiven of sin?

A: As often as we sincerely repent.

Perhaps you are concerned that you keep repenting of the same things, and it is beginning to make you feel like a hypocrite to keep asking for forgiveness. One of the most powerful aspects of the Atonement is that it is specifically designed to help us in daily living, rather than being reserved only for gross sin. Because it is formulated by God to help us progress and improve in everyday life, it is to be expected that we will encounter a number of weaknesses and imperfections that require continuous effort to overcome. A key issue, then, is that we avoid excessive discouragement and continue trying. Thus, it should not surprise us if we repent sincerely, time and time again, of some sins, before we finally succeed in overcoming them. Sincerity, as you can no doubt see, is a key to this process. The Lord explains His willingness to forgive over and over upon sincere repentance as follows:

> **Mosiah 26:29–30**
>
> 29 Therefore I say unto you, Go; and whosoever transgresseth against me, him shall ye judge according to the sins which he has committed; and if he confess his sins before thee and me, **and repenteth in the sincerity of his heart,** him shall ye forgive, and I will forgive him also.
>
> 30 Yea, and **as often as my people repent will I forgive them** their trespasses against me.

Q: Does the Atonement of Jesus Christ apply to our world alone or to other worlds also?

A: Other worlds also.

The answer to this question is given in the Doctrine and Covenants:

D&C 76:24

24 That by him [Christ], and through him, and of him, the **worlds** [note that this is plural] are and were created, and **the inhabitants thereof** [of all the Father's worlds] **are begotten sons and daughters unto God** [are given the opportunity to gain exaltation].

In case there is any question as to whether we understand the above verse correctly, we will also include a quote from Elder Bruce R. McConkie, as used in the *Doctrines of the Gospel Student Manual*, 1986 edition:

Bruce R. McConkie

"Now our Lord's jurisdiction and power extend far beyond the limits of this one small earth on which we dwell. He is, under the Father, the Creator of **worlds without number.** (Moses 1:33.) And through the power of his atonement the inhabitants of these worlds, the revelation says, 'are begotten sons and daughters unto God' (D&C 76:24), which means that the **atonement of Christ, being literally and truly infinite, applies to an infinite number of earths.**

"Those who have ears to hear, find this doctrine taught in the following scripture: 'And we beheld the glory of the Son, on the right hand of the Father, and received of his fulness,' the Prophet says in recording the Vision, 'And saw the holy angels, and them who are sanctified before his throne, worshiping God, and the Lamb, who worship him forever and ever. And now, after the many testimonies which have been given of him, this is the testimony, last of all, which we give of him: That he lives! For we saw him, even on the right hand of God; and we heard the voice bearing record that he is the Only Begotten of the Father—That by him, and through him, and of him, the worlds are and were created, and the inhabitants thereof are begotten sons and daughters unto God.'

(D&C 76:20–24.)

"In addition to the plain meaning of this passage, we have an explanation of it given by the Prophet Joseph Smith. He paraphrased, in poetical rhyme, the entire record of the Vision [D&C 76], and his words covering this portion were:

"'I beheld round the throne holy angels and hosts,
And *sanctified beings from worlds that have been,*
In holiness worshipping God and the Lamb,
For ever and ever. Amen and amen. . . .

"'And I heard a great voice bearing record from heav'n,
He's the Saviour *and Only Begotten of God;*
By him, of him, and through him, the worlds were all made,
Even all that careen in the heavens so broad.

"'**Whose inhabitants, too, from the first to the last,**
Are sav'd by the very same Saviour of ours;
And, of course, are begotten God's daughters and sons
By the very same truths and the very same powers.'
(*Millennial Star,* vol. 4, pp. 49–55.)"

(*Mormon Doctrine,* 65–66; see also *Doctrines of the Gospel Student Manual,* 25–26).

Q: If we become gods, will our Savior's Atonement work for our worlds also?

A: We don't know for sure. An authoritative answer has not yet been given by a prophet.

In conclusion, the Atonement of Jesus Christ permeates every aspect of our lives. It is the means by which we can be cleansed from sin and inadequacy. It is a gift of the Father to His children through which they can return pure and clean and be comfortable and secure in His presence forever. It harmonizes the laws of justice and mercy perfectly, and it allows us to exercise our agency within a completely secure framework. Thus, it gives us the opportunity, if we so choose, of pressing forward "with a steadfastness in Christ, having a perfect brightness of hope" (2 Nephi 31:20), that we can and will obtain eternal life.

CHAPTER SIX

MORTALITY—OUR LIFE ON EARTH

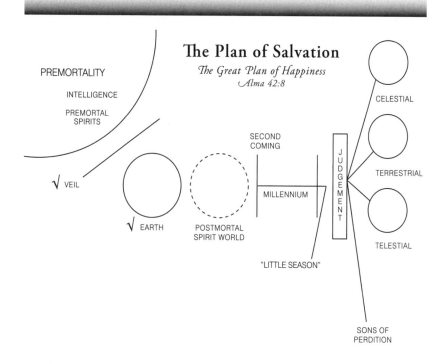

The Plan of Salvation

The Great Plan of Happiness
Alma 42:8

PREMORTALITY

INTELLIGENCE

PREMORTAL
SPIRITS

√ VEIL

√ EARTH

POSTMORTAL
SPIRIT WORLD

SECOND
COMING

MILLENNIUM

"LITTLE SEASON"

JUDGEMENT

CELESTIAL

TERRESTRIAL

TELESTIAL

SONS OF
PERDITION

We will briefly consider a number of aspects of mortality. In a significant sense, we have been sent away from home to the "University of Earth" to continue our education toward becoming like our Father in Heaven. Before coming to earth, we were schooled for eons in our premortal life. We progressed much and were prepared in terms of character development and knowledge of the Plan of Salvation. We might say that we successfully completed kindergarten through high school and received bachelor's and master's degrees in premortality and that we have now been sent away to earth to work on our Ph.D.—exaltation. We will discuss this more as we go along in this chapter, but first we will briefly consider the "veil" that has been drawn over the memory of our premortal life.

Q: Why do we have the veil?

A: It is a vital part of our progression toward exaltation.

The veil has several functions, including the following:
- It separates us from "home."
- It lets us find out how we will behave when we feel more on our own.
- It allows our character to be tested.
- It allows our character to be developed much more.
- It requires that we seek contact with our Father (agency).
- It allows greater depth and growth in the exercise of agency.

Q: Does the veil filter out everything about our premortal life?

A: No.

The veil removes our specific memory of the premortal life, but it does not filter out our personalities, talents, needs for further development, and so forth. For instance, perhaps you've noticed that babies come through the veil with well-developed personalities. Also, we sometimes have inklings or flashes of memory that reach back to our pre-earth life and that seem to be available to all people on occasions. For example, as missionaries are preaching the gospel to prospective members, these investigators sometimes sense or feel that they've heard the doctrine before. They have indeed, in the premortal spirit world. President Joseph F. Smith spoke of these glimpses of our former life (**bold** added for emphasis):

Joseph F. Smith
"We often catch a spark from the awakened **memories** of the immortal soul, which lights up our whole being as with the **glory of our former home**" (*Gospel Doctrine*, 14).

President Joseph Fielding Smith also addressed this subject concerning things the veil does not remove:

Joseph Fielding Smith
"The characteristics of the spirit which were developed through many ages of a former existence play a very important part in our progression through mortal life" (*Improvement Era*, March 1916, 426).

Purposes of Earth Life

We have been sent to earth for many purposes. We will list some of these in a minute. As previously mentioned, in a significant sense, we could refer to this stage of our schooling as the "University of Earth." We have already completed much education as spirits and have "graduated" from premortality. Now we have been sent away from home, down to this earth to enter the final stage of our education. We have, in effect, passed the entrance exams and qualified to attend the advanced education courses available on the University of Earth. If we keep our focus here and study and work faithfully, we will "graduate" on final

Judgment Day with our degree in exaltation. President Spencer W. Kimball spoke of this schooling as follows:

Spencer W. Kimball

"You are sent to this world with a very serious purpose. **You are sent to school** . . . to begin as a human infant and grow to unbelievable proportions in wisdom, judgement, knowledge, and power . . . and prepare for the later life when limitations will terminate so that we can go on and on and on" (*Doctrines of the Gospel Student Manual*, 29).

Some Purposes of Mortality

- Gain a physical body (Genesis 2:7; D&C 88:15). Having a physical body opens the door for a "fullness of joy" (D&C 93:33; 138:17).
- Have joy (2 Nephi 2:25; Moses 5:10–11).
- Be tested (Abraham 3:25)
- Learn to appreciate the good by tasting the bitter (2 Nephi 2:15, 23; D&C 29:39; Moses 6:55).
- Learn to walk by faith (Galatians 2:20; Romans 1:17; D&C 88:118).
- Learn to use the Atonement of Christ in our daily lives to continue growing and progressing (Acts 17:28).

Q: Why is a physical body so important?

A: Without one, we cannot become like our Father in Heaven.

One of the most important purposes of mortality is to gain a physical body of flesh and bones. Without this mortal body, we would be stopped in our progression to become like our Father in Heaven, who has a glorious, resurrected, physical body of "flesh and bones as tangible as man's" (D&C 130:22). The Prophet

Joseph Smith taught that obtaining a physical body is a vital part of the Plan of Salvation and is essential to our eternal happiness.

Joseph Smith

"We came to this earth that we might have a body and present it pure before God in the celestial kingdom. **The great principle of happiness consists in having a body**" (*Teachings of the Prophet Joseph Smith*, 181).

Joseph Fielding Smith spoke of our desire in the premortal world of spirits to obtain a glorious, resurrected body of flesh and bones like the one possessed by our Father in Heaven:

Joseph Fielding Smith

"At one time we were in the presence of our Eternal Father. There is not a soul in this room, not one, that has not seen him. You do not remember it, I do not remember it, but nevertheless there was a time before we ever came into this world when we dwelt in his presence. We knew what kind of a being he is. One thing we saw was how glorious he is. Another thing, how great was his wisdom, his understanding, how wonderful was his power and his inspiration. And **we wanted to be like him.** And because we wanted to be like him, we are here. We could not be like him and stay in his presence, because **we did not have glorious bodies of flesh and bones.** We were just spirits, and the spirit does not have flesh and bones. But we saw him in his glory and it was made known to us that by keeping his commandments and observing every covenant that would be given to us on this earth, we could come back again into his presence, receiving our bodies in the resurrection from the dead—our spirits and bodies being united again, inseparably, never again to be divided.

"If we will just be true and faithful to every covenant, to every principle of truth that he has given us, then after the resurrection we would come back into his presence and we would be just like he is. We would have the same kind of bodies—bodies that would shine like the sun" (*Take Heed to Yourselves!* 345; see *also Doctrines of the Gospel Student Manual*, 28).

Q: Can we be tempted here on earth beyond our ability to resist?

A: No (1 Corinthians 10:13).

Elder Joseph B. Wirthlin addressed this important subject as follows:

Joseph B. Wirthlin

"I suppose some of you, at one time or another, feel that you are 'hitting the wall,' feeling an almost compelling urge to quit, give up, or give in to temptation. You will meet challenges, adversities, and temptations that seem to be more than you can bear. In times of sickness, death, financial need, and other hardships, you many wonder whether you have the strength, courage, or ability to continue. . . . Be sure you understand that God will not allow you to be tempted beyond your ability to resist. (See 1 Corinthians 10:13.) He does not give you challenges that you cannot surmount. He will not ask more than you can do, but may ask right up to your limits so you can prove yourselves" ("Running Your Marathon," *Ensign*, November 1989, 74–75).

Q: Does the Atonement work for our inadequacies and imperfections as well as our sins?

A: Yes.

Neal A. Maxwell

"In Alma 7:12, the only place in scriptures, to my knowledge, that it appears, there seems to have been yet another purpose of the Atonement, speaking again of the Savior and his suffering, 'and He will take upon him death, that he may loose the bands of death which bind his people; and he will take upon him their infirmities, that his bowels may be filled with mercy. . . .' Have you ever thought that there was no way that Jesus could know the suffering which we undergo as a result of our stupidity and sin (because he was sinless) except he bear those sins of ours in what I call the awful arithmetic of the Atonement?" (*Symposium on the Old Testament*, 17; see also *Doctrines of the Gospel Student Manual*, 24–25).

Q: Sometimes our imperfections can become pretty discouraging here on earth. If we keep trying with a sincere heart, will we be allowed to continue progressing after we die?

A: Yes.

Some members of the Church seem to get mixed up between the words "perfect" and "spotless." They are not the same. Because Christ was the only perfect person who has ever lived on earth, we obviously cannot be perfect at the time of death. However, we can be spotless, meaning that we can live worthily for the Savior's Atonement to make us completely clean from sin by the time of the final judgment. Being thus made spotless, we can continue progressing in the next life until we become perfect.

Therefore, the next question is, "How can we qualify to be made spotless in order to continue progressing until we become perfect?" The answer is found in Alma 34. We will quote a verse from this chapter and use **bold** to emphasize a key word that will answer the question:

Alma 34:33

33 And now, as I said unto you before, as ye have had so many witnesses, therefore, I beseech of you that ye do not procrastinate the day of your repentance until the end; for after this day of life, which is given us to prepare for eternity, behold, if we do not **improve** our time while in this life, then cometh the night of darkness wherein there can be no labor performed.

The answer, then, is found in the word "improve." If we sincerely try to keep improving, we enable the Savior to make us completely clean, or "spotless." Thus, we become worthy to return to the presence of God and to continue progressing until we attain perfection. Another verse from the same chapter of Alma confirms this.

Alma 34:36

36 And this I know, because the Lord hath said he dwelleth not in unholy temples, but in the hearts of the righteous doth he dwell; yea, and he has also said that **the righteous shall sit down in his kingdom,** to go no more out; but their garments should be **made white through the blood of the Lamb.**

Elder Dallin H. Oaks addressed this same issue of our imperfection despite our efforts to honestly and sincerely live the gospel:

Dallin H. Oaks

"Another idea that is powerful to lift us from discouragement is that the work of the Church . . . is an eternal work. Not all problems . . . are fixed in mortality. The work of salvation goes on beyond the veil of death, and we should not be too apprehensive about incompleteness within the limits of mortality" ("Powerful Ideas," *Ensign,* November 1995, 26).

Q: Great blessings have been promised to "the righteous" (2 Nephi 9:18). Who are the righteous?

A: The righteous are sinners who are repenting, striving to be righteous, and continuing to improve. The wicked are sinners who don't repent or strive to be righteous.

The key issue is that we honestly and sincerely strive to keep the commandments and do better each day. Elder Spencer W. Kimball reminded us that our progress toward perfection can actually be quite rapid if we sincerely work at it:

Spencer W. Kimball

"Men do not suddenly become righteous any more than a tiny acorn suddenly becomes an oak. Advancement to perfection can nevertheless be rapid if one resolutely strides toward the goal" (*The Miracle of Forgiveness*, 210).

Having taken a brief look at the phase or stage of the "great plan of happiness" (Alma 42:8) in which we now find ourselves as mortals, we will move on to the next stage, namely, the spirit world. Unless the Millennium comes during our lifetime, we will all die and enter the spirit world to await the Second Coming of Christ and the work that will be done during the thousand years of His millennial reign. There is much going on in the spirit world right now.

CHAPTER SEVEN

THE POSTMORTAL SPIRIT WORLD

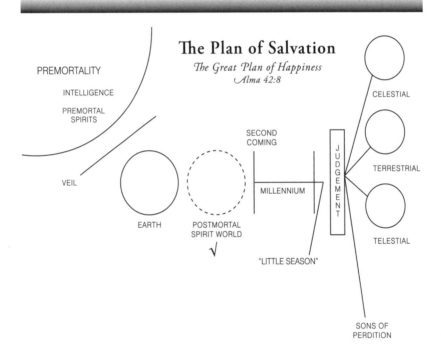

The Plan of Salvation

The Great Plan of Happiness
Alma 42:8

PREMORTALITY

INTELLIGENCE

PREMORTAL SPIRITS

VEIL

EARTH

POSTMORTAL SPIRIT WORLD

SECOND COMING

MILLENNIUM

"LITTLE SEASON"

JUDGEMENT

CELESTIAL

TERRESTRIAL

TELESTIAL

SONS OF PERDITION

The scriptures inform us that when we die, we lay our mortal body aside temporarily until we are resurrected and our spirit enters the postmortal spirit world. The book of Alma teaches this doctrine as follows:

Alma 40:11

11 Now, concerning the state of the soul between death and the resurrection—Behold, it has been made known unto me by an angel, that the spirits of all men, as soon as they are departed from this mortal body, yea, the spirits of all men, whether they be good or evil, are taken home to that God who gave them life.

Joseph F. Smith expounded on this doctrine in 1914:

Joseph F. Smith

"The spirits of all men, as soon as they depart from this mortal body, whether they are good or evil, we are told in the Book of Mormon, are taken home to that God who gave them life, where there is a separation, a partial judgment, and the spirits of those who are righteous are received into a state of happiness which is called paradise, a state of rest, a state of peace, where they expand in wisdom, where they have respite from all their troubles, and where care and sorrow do not annoy. The wicked, on the contrary, have no part nor portion in the Spirit of the Lord, and they are cast into outer darkness [the prison portion of the spirit world], being led captive, because of their own iniquity, by the evil one. And in this space between death and the resurrection of the body, the two classes of souls remain, in happiness or in misery, until the time which is appointed of God that the dead shall come forth and be reunited both spirit and body, and be brought to stand before God, and be judged according to their works. This is the final judgment" (*Improvement Era*, vol. 7, June 1914, 619; see also Smith, *Gospel Doctrine*, 448).

In 1918, shortly before his death, President Smith had a marvelous vision of the redemption of the dead and the great missionary work that is going on in the spirit world. From this vision, now known as section 138 of the Doctrine and Covenants, we gain many more details about the postmortal spirit world. One of the most important doctrinal details is that the gospel is being taught extensively in the spirit prison (D&C 138:30–37). Thus, for our purposes, we will often refer to "spirit prison" as the "spirit world mission field." We will continue by asking several questions about this spirit world.

Q: Is the postmortal spirit world the same as the premortal spirit world?

A: No.

We have been taught that the postmortal spirit world is not the same as the premortal spirit world. While there are obvious instances where spirit beings from both spheres have contact with each other—such as when the spirit of a baby who is soon to be born sees the spirit of a grandparent, sibling, or other family member who has just died—we are taught that they are two separate places. Keep in mind that the premortal spirit children of God live with Him as they are raised and taught in preparation for being sent to earth. In the manual for Relief Society and priesthood study published in 1997 by the Church, we read the following:

Brigham Young
"Spirits, when they leave their bodies, do not dwell with the Father and the Son, but live in the Spirit world, where there are places prepared for them" (*Teachings of the Presidents of the Church—Brigham Young*, 276–77).

Q: Do we know where the postmortal spirit world is?

A: Yes.

Both the Prophet Joseph Smith and Brigham Young revealed information regarding the location of the spirit world. We will provide a quote from each of them. Joseph Smith spoke of the righteous who have died and gone to the world of spirits (**bold** is used for emphasis):

Joseph Smith
"Enveloped in flaming fire, **they are not far from us,** and know and understand our thoughts, feelings, and motions, and are often pained therewith" (*Teachings of the Prophet Joseph Smith*, 326).

Brigham Young
"When you lay down this tabernacle, where are you going? Into the spiritual world. Are you going into Abraham's bosom? No, not anywhere nigh there [Abraham has already been resurrected and become a god (D&C 133:55; D&C 132:37)] but into the spirit world. **Where is the spirit world? It is right here**" (*Discourses of Brigham Young*, 376).

Q: How many divisions are there in the spirit world?

A: Two—paradise and prison.

Paradise

Alma 40:12
12 And then shall it come to pass, that the spirits of those who are righteous are received into a state of

happiness, which is called paradise, a state of rest, a state of peace, where they shall rest from all their troubles and from all care, and sorrow.

Prison (mission field)

1 Peter 3:18–20

18 For Christ also hath once suffered for sins, the just for the unjust, that he might bring us to God, being put to death in the flesh, but quickened by the Spirit:

19 By which also he went and preached unto the spirits in prison.

Q: What is paradise?

A: The place where righteous people go when they die.

Bruce R. McConkie

"Paradise—the abode of righteous spirits, as they await the day of their resurrection; paradise—a place of peace and rest where the sorrows and trials of his life have been shuffled off, and where the saints continue to prepare for a celestial heaven; paradise—not the Lord's eternal kingdom, but a way station along the course leading to eternal life, a place where the final preparation is made for that fulness of joy which comes only when body and spirit are inseparably connected in immortal glory! Thither Jesus this day is going. And in that general realm—the realm of departed spirits—so also will the so-called penitent thief find himself. He will not this day sit down on a throne on the right side of the Lord; even James and John were denied an assurance of such a reward. He will not stand in the congregation of the righteous when Jesus meets with Adam and Noah and Abraham and all the righteous dead; but he will be in the realm of the departed where he can learn from the Lord's legal administrators all that he must do to work out his salvation. If we had the most accurate possible translation, one that conveyed Jesus' real intent, his words to his fellow crucifee would convey this thought: 'This day shalt thou be with me in the world of spirits. There you can learn of me and my gospel; there you can begin to work out your salvation with fear and trembling before me'" (*The Mortal Messiah*, 4:222).

Q: Who goes to paradise?

A: Children who die before the age of accountability, as well as faithful, baptized members of the Church.

Paradise is a place reserved for the righteous who have accepted the gospel, lived it faithfully, and are continuing in their progression toward glory in the celestial kingdom. Obviously, children who die before the age of accountability also go to paradise. In addition, these righteous postmortal spirits are called upon to teach the gospel as missionaries in the prison portion of the spirit world, or what we are referring to as the "spirit world mission field."

Joseph Fielding Smith explained that righteous, faithful, baptized members of the Church are the ones who go to paradise:

Joseph Fielding Smith

"As I understand it, *the righteous—meaning those who have been baptized and who have been faithful—*are **gathered in one part** and **all the others in another part of the spirit world.** This seems to be true from the vision given to President Joseph F. Smith [see D&C 138]" (*Doctrines of Salvation*, 2:230).

Q: What is life after death like for the righteous when they die and go to paradise?

A: It will be wonderful for all and a great relief for those who have been ill and suffered physically before they died.

President Brigham Young described it this way:

Brigham Young

"We shall turn round and look upon it [the valley of death] and think, when we have crossed it, why this is the greatest advantage of my whole existence, for I have passed from a state of sorrow, grief, mourning, woe, misery, pain, anguish and disappointment into a state of existence, where I can enjoy life to the fullest extent as far as that can be done without a body. My spirit is set free, I thirst no more, I want to sleep no more, I hunger no more, I tire no more, I run, I walk, I labor, I go, I come, I do this, I do that, whatever is required of me, nothing like pain or weariness, I am full of life, full of vigor, and I enjoy the presence of my heavenly Father" (in *Journal of Discourses*, 17:142; see also *Doctrines of the Gospel Student Manual*, 83).

Q: What is spirit prison?

A: The portion of the postmortal spirit world where all go except faithful Latter-day Saints and children who die before the age of accountability.

Q: Why is it called "prison?"

A: All who go there, whether wicked or good, are limited in their progression because they do not have or have not accepted the redeeming gospel of Jesus Christ.

Thus, they are, in effect, behind bars and limited in their progress until they accept the covenants and principles of the gospel that open the door to celestial glory and eternal progression.

Q: Does that mean that there are good people in the spirit prison mission field?

A: Yes.

Only children who die before the age of accountability and faithful, baptized members of the Church go to paradise (see above quote by Joseph Fielding Smith). See also Doctrine and Covenants 138:32, which says, "Thus was the gospel preached to those who had died in their sins, without a knowledge of the truth."

In other words, the spirit world mission field, or spirit prison, is much like being on this earth. Here, we all live in the mission field. There are many good and honorable people who are not members of the Church who desire the truth but who have not had a complete opportunity to hear, understand, and accept the gospel. Likewise, there are many wicked who are intentionally evil. The sincere and good spirits who accept the gospel when they hear and understand it in the spirit prison, as well as the wicked postmortal spirits who repent (see D&C 138:32), will receive every privilege and blessing of the gospel via temple work done for them by mortals.

This doctrine is comforting to those who worry about good and honorable loved ones and friends who have died but are not yet in paradise. They realize that these loved ones are not being punished by being sent to the spirit prison, or mission field; rather, they are being given an opportunity to hear, understand, and accept the gospel, just as is the case with people on earth. Furthermore, they must accept it in an environment of opposition and diversity of belief systems, just as we here on earth must. If they accept it and are faithful there, they will have every opportunity of obtaining the highest degree of glory in the celestial kingdom once their temple work is done by mortals—either now or during the Millennium.

Q: It confuses me when I read that the gospel is being taught to the "wicked" in prison. I understand that there are also good people in the spirit world mission field too. Is there more than one definition of the word "wicked" as used in this context?

A: Yes.

The word "wicked" is most often used to describe those who are defiant and evil, intentionally breaking the commandments of God and engaging in intentional conduct that destroys society and civilization. However, it can also mean those who do not have the gospel. This is the case in one context of the following scripture:

D&C 84:51–53

51 For **whoso cometh not unto me is under the bondage of sin.**

52 And **whoso** receiveth not my voice **is not acquainted with my voice,** and is not of me.

53 And by this you may know the righteous from the **wicked,** and that the whole world groaneth under sin and darkness even now.

Thus, the term "wicked" can simply mean those who are not yet acquainted with the gospel of Christ. There are many such good people dwell in the postmortal spirit world, as well as here on earth. This same concept is taught in a footnote found in *The Teachings of the Prophet Joseph Smith*:

Teachings of the Prophet Joseph Smith

"In using the term **'wicked men'** . . . the Prophet did so in the same sense in which the Lord uses it in the eighty-fourth section of the Doctrine and Covenants, [verses] 49–53. The Lord in this scripture speaks of **those who have not received the gospel** as being under the bondage of sin, and hence 'wicked.' However, **many of these people are honorable, clean living men,** but they have not embraced the Gospel. The inhabitants of the terrestrial order will remain on the earth during the Millennium, and this class are without the Gospel ordinances" (*Teachings of the Prophet Joseph Smith,* 269 n. 2).

Q: I thought the thief on the cross went to paradise, and he wasn't a member of Christ's church. So why would the Savior say to him, "To day shalt thou be with me in paradise" (Luke 23:43)?

A: This is an example of where the Bible is not translated correctly. In fact, it is a good example of the eighth article of faith, which states, "We believe the Bible to be the word of God as far as it is translated correctly."

The Bible Dictionary answers this question as follows:

Bible Dictionary
"The Bible rendering is incorrect. The statement would more accurately read, 'Today shalt thou be with me in the world of spirits' since the thief was not ready for paradise" (see "paradise").

Q: Can Satan and his evil spirits tempt in the spirit world?

A: No and yes.

They cannot tempt the righteous spirits who have gone to paradise, but they can tempt in the spirit prison mission field, just as they tempt people here on earth. President Brigham Young said:

Brigham Young

"If we are faithful to our religion, when we go into the spirit world, the fallen spirits—Lucifer and the third part of the heavenly hosts that came with him, and the spirits of wicked men who have dwelt upon this earth . . . will have no influence over our spirits. . . . All the rest of the children of men are more or less subject to them, and they are subject to them as they were while here in the flesh" (*Teachings of the Presidents of the Church—Brigham Young*, 282).

Q: We know from D&C 138:57 that faithful elders who have died will preach the gospel in the spirit prison mission field. Will righteous sisters be missionaries also?

A: Yes.

Joseph F. Smith

"Now among all these millions of spirits that have lived on the earth and have passed away . . . without the knowledge of the gospel—among them you may count that at least one-half are women. Who is going to preach the gospel to the women? . . . These good sisters . . . will be fully authorized and empowered to preach the gospel and minister to the women while the elders and prophets are preaching it to the men" (*Gospel Doctrine*, 461).

CHAPTER EIGHT

THE SECOND COMING

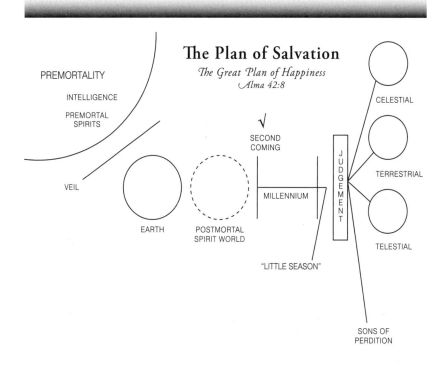

The Plan of Salvation
The Great Plan of Happiness
Alma 42:8

PREMORTALITY

INTELLIGENCE

PREMORTAL
SPIRITS

VEIL

EARTH

POSTMORTAL
SPIRIT WORLD

SECOND
COMING

MILLENNIUM

"LITTLE SEASON"

JUDGEMENT

CELESTIAL

TERRESTRIAL

TELESTIAL

SONS OF
PERDITION

The Second Coming of Jesus Christ is a much-anticipated event. It has been prophesied many, many times and is the subject of much discussion and interest. As members of the Church, with access to both ancient and modern scripture, as well as the words and teachings of modern prophets, seers, and revelators, we are in a position to know a considerable amount about this major event in the Plan of Salvation. We will first take a brief look at some "comings" of the Savior that are not the Second Coming.

Major Appearances of the Savior before the Second Coming

The following appearances of the Savior are not necessarily listed in sequence:

1. To those in the New Jerusalem in America (3 Nephi 21:23–25; D&C 45:66–67).
2. To the Jews in Jerusalem (D&C 45:48, 51–53; Zechariah 12:10; 14:2–5).
3. To those assembled at Adam-ondi-Ahman (Daniel 7:9–10, 13–14; D&C 116).

Bruce R. McConkie

"We now come to the least known and least understood thing connected with the second coming. . . . It is a doctrine that has scarcely dawned on most of the Latter-day Saints themselves. . . . Before the Lord Jesus descends openly . . . there is to be a secret appearance to selected members of His Church. He will come in private to his prophet and to the apostles then living . . . and further, all the faithful members of the Church then living and all the faithful saints of all the ages past will be present . . . and it will take place in Davies County, Missouri, at a place called Adam-ondi-Ahman. . . . The grand summation of the whole matter comes in these words: 'and also with all

those whom my Father hath given me out of the world'
(D&C 27:14). The sacrament is to be administered . . . this,
of course, will be a part of the Grand Council at Adam-
ondi-Ahman" (*The Millennial Messiah*, 578–79, 587).

The Actual Second Coming

Q: What will happen to the faithful Saints?

A: They will be taken up alive to meet the coming Lord.

D&C 88:96

96 And the saints that are upon the earth, who are
alive, shall be quickened and be caught up to meet him:

Q: Who is resurrected at His coming?

A: Those in the grave who are worthy of celestial glory.

D&C 88:97

97 And they who have slept in their graves shall come
forth, for their graves shall be opened; and they also shall
be caught up to meet him in the midst of the pillar of
heaven—

Q: What color will He be wearing and why?

**A: Red, symbolizing the blood of the unrepentant wicked,
who now must answer to the law of justice, having
refused the law of mercy offered through the Atonement.**

Whether the Savior's clothing is literally red or symbolically red, the imagery is the same. The color represents the blood of the wicked who are destroyed at His coming, as indicated below, with **bold** added for emphasis.

D&C 133:46–51

46 And it shall be said: Who is this that cometh down from God in **heaven with dyed garments** [with dyed clothing]; yea, from the regions which are not known, clothed in his glorious apparel, traveling in the greatness of his strength?

47 And he shall say: I am he who spake in righteousness, mighty to save.

48 **And the Lord shall be red in his apparel** [clothing], and his garments like him that treadeth in the wine-vat [like one who has been treading grapes in the wine tub].

49 And so great shall be the glory of his presence that the sun shall hide his face in shame, and the moon shall withhold its light, and the stars shall be hurled from their places.

50 And his voice shall be heard: I have trodden the wine-press alone, and have brought judgment upon all people; and none were with me [Jesus had to do the Atonement alone];

51 And I have trampled them [the wicked] in my fury, and I did tread upon them in mine anger, **and their blood have I sprinkled upon my garments, and stained all my raiment** [clothing]; for this was the day of vengeance [the law of justice is being satisfied] which was in my heart [which is part of the Plan of Salvation that the Savior is carrying out for the Father, along with the law of mercy].

Q: From what direction will He Come?

A: From the east.

Joseph Smith–Matthew 1:26

26 For as the light of the morning cometh out of the east, and shineth even unto the west, and covereth the whole earth, so shall also the coming of the Son of Man be.

Q: How will the wicked be destroyed?

A: By the glory of the Lord as He comes to earth.

D&C 5:19

19 For a desolating scourge shall go forth among the inhabitants of the earth, and shall continue to be poured out from time to time, if they repent not, until the earth is empty, and the inhabitants thereof are consumed away and **utterly destroyed by the brightness of my coming.**

2 Nephi 12:10, 19, 21

10 O ye wicked ones, enter into the rock, and hide thee in the dust, for the fear of the Lord and **the glory of his majesty shall smite thee.**

19 And they shall go into the holes of the rocks, and into the caves of the earth, for the fear of the Lord shall come upon them **and the glory of his majesty shall smite them,** when he ariseth to shake terribly the earth.

21 To go into the clefts of the rocks, and into the tops of the ragged rocks, for the fear of the Lord shall come upon them and **the majesty of his glory shall smite them,** when he ariseth to shake terribly the earth [perhaps referring to the moving of the continents back together, in conjunction with the Second Coming].

Q: What will happen to the earth?

A: The continents will be moved back together, and the earth will be restored to a condition such as in the Garden of Eden (see Articles of Faith 1:10, footnote f). In other words, it will receive its "paradisiacal glory" in preparation for the Millennium.

D&C 133:23

23 He shall command the great deep, and it shall be driven back into the north countries, and the islands shall become one land.

Articles of Faith 1:10

10 We believe in the literal gathering of Israel and in the restoration of the Ten Tribes; that Zion (the New Jerusalem) will be built upon the American continent; that Christ will reign personally upon the earth; and, that **the earth will be renewed and receive its paradisiacal glory.**

Q: Who will come with the Savior when he returns?

A: The hosts of heaven plus the righteous who have just been resurrected and the righteous mortals who have just been caught up to meet Him.

D&C 88:96–98

96 And **the saints** that are **upon the earth, who are alive,** shall be quickened [made capable of bearing the presence of the Lord with their mortal bodies] and be caught up to meet him.

97 And they [the righteous] **who have slept in their graves** shall come forth, for their graves shall be opened; and they also shall be caught up to meet him in the midst of the pillar of heaven—

98 **They are Christ's,** the first fruits, **they who shall descend with him first,** and they who are on the earth [the righteous Saints who are still alive] and in their graves [the righteous dead who have just been resurrected], who are first caught up to meet him; and all this by the voice of the sounding of the trump of the angel of God.

Q: Will everyone be caught off guard when Christ's coming occurs like "a thief in the night" (D&C 106:4)?

A: No. The righteous will be ready and will know that His coming is getting close. However, the wicked will be caught off guard.

D&C 106:4–5

4 And again, verily I say unto you, **the coming of the Lord draweth nigh** [is getting close], and **it overtaketh the world** [the wicked] as a thief in the night—

5 Therefore, gird up your loins [get ready], that you may be the children of light [that you may be counted among the righteous], and **that day** [the Second Coming] **shall not overtake you as a thief.**

Q: How will the wicked feel at the Second Coming?

A: They will wish they could die and somehow avoid facing the Savior.

Revelation 6:16–17

16 And [they] said to the mountains and rocks, **Fall on us, and hide us** from the face of him that sitteth on the throne, and from the wrath of the Lamb:

17 For the great day of his wrath is come; and who shall be able to stand?

Q: Will our prophets tell us the exact time of the Savior's coming?

A: No.

Matthew 24:36

36 But of that day and hour knoweth no man, no, not the angels of heaven, but my Father only.

Mark 13:32

32 But of that day and that hour knoweth **no man,** no, **not the angels** which are in heaven, **neither the Son,** but the Father.

D&C 49:7

7 I, the Lord God, have spoken it; but the hour and the day no man knoweth, neither the angels in heaven, **nor shall they know until he comes.**

Q: Will things get better between now and the Second Coming?

A: No.

D&C 84:97

97 And plagues shall go forth, and they shall not be taken from the earth until I have completed my work, which shall be cut short in righteousness.

D&C 97:23

23 The Lord's scourge shall pass over by night and by day, and the report thereof shall vex all people; yea, it shall not be stayed [restrained, stopped] until the Lord come.

Q: As we see the signs of the times being fulfilled all around us, should we panic?

A: No.

The Savior made it clear to his disciples that the purpose of the "signs of the times" (prophecies of the Second Coming) was not to promote panic. Rather, they are given to strengthen the testimonies of the faithful as they see the prophecies fulfilled. We will quote the Master as He taught His disciples on this matter:

Joseph Smith–Matthew 1:23, 37, 39

23 Behold, I speak these things [the signs of the times] unto you for the elect's sake; and you also shall hear of wars, and rumors of wars; **see that ye be not troubled,** for all I have told you must come to pass; but the end is not yet.

37 And **whoso treasureth up my word, shall not be deceived,** for the Son of Man shall come, and he shall send his angels before him with the great sound of a trumpet, and they shall gather together the remainder of his elect from the four winds, from one end of heaven to the other.

39 So likewise, **mine elect, when they shall see all these things, they shall know that he is near, even at the doors.**

Q: What are the "signs of the times"?

A: They are prophecies telling of things that will take place indicating that the Second Coming is getting close.

Q: What are some of the signs of the times?

A: The following is a list of thirty-seven such prophecies.

37 Signs of the Times

1. America is discovered and the United States of America is established (1 Nephi 22:7; 3 Nephi 21:4).

2. The Book of Mormon comes forth (Ezekiel 37:16–19).

3. The priesthood is restored (Malachi 4:4–6).

4. The true Church is restored (Acts 3:19–21).

5. The Church grows to fill the whole earth (Daniel 2:35, 44–45).

6. Scattered Israel is gathered (1 Nephi 10:14).

7. The lost ten tribes return (D&C 133:26–34).

8. The times of the Gentiles are fulfilled (D&C 45:25).

9. The Jews return to Jerusalem (D&C 133:13).

10. The Jews accept the true gospel (2 Nephi 30:7).

11. Elijah comes (Malachi 4:5–6).

12. Christ comes to His temple (Malachi 3:1).

13. Family history research increases dramatically (Malachi 4:6).

14. The sun is darkened and the moon becomes as blood (Matthew 24:29; Revelation 6:12; Joel 2:28–32).

15. Diseases, plagues, and pestilences sweep the earth (D&C 45:31; Joseph Smith–Matthew 1:29).

16. Knowledge and science increase dramatically (Daniel 12:4).

17. Wars and rumors of wars abound (D&C 45:26; Joseph Smith–Matthew 1:23).

18. Famines, tornadoes, earthquakes, and natural disasters abound (D&C 45:26).

19. Strikes, anarchy, and violence increase (McConkie, *Mormon Doctrine*, 726).

20. Sexual immorality, homosexuality, and other perversions

abound (2 Timothy 3:3, 6).

21. The Spirit is withheld from the wicked (D&C 63:32).

22. Peace is taken from the earth (D&C 1:35).

23. Jerusalem becomes a "cup of trembling" to people around it (Zechariah 12:2).

24. False churches and false prophets abound (Revelation 13:13–14).

25. Many people refuse to believe the signs of the times (2 Peter 3:3–4).

26. Signs and wonders occur on earth and in the heavens (D&C 45:40).

27. The Lamanites blossom as the rose (D&C 49:24).

28. The New Jerusalem is built (Moses 7:63–64).

29. Many temples are built (Ezra Taft Benson, "A Marvelous Work and a Wonder," *Ensign*, May 1980, 33; Bruce R. Mc-Conkie, "The Coming Tests and Trials and Glory," *Ensign*, May 1980, 72).

30. A temple is built in Jerusalem (*Teachings of the Prophet Joseph Smith*, 286).

31. The battle of Armageddon occurs (Zechariah 12).

32. An important meeting is held at Adam-ondi-Ahman (Daniel 7:9–14).

33. Two prophets are killed in Jerusalem (Revelation 11).

34. The Mount of Olives divides in two (Zechariah 14:4).

35. The righteous are taken up (D&C 88:96).

36. The wicked are burned (Malachi 4:1; 2 Nephi 12:10, 19, 21; D&C 5:19).

37. Everyone alive sees Christ coming (Revelation 1:7).

Resurrection

As you are probably already aware, there will be a major resurrection of the righteous in conjunction with the Second Coming. This is spoken of many times in scripture. In 1 Corinthians, Paul teaches us that Christ will be the first one resurrected and that there will be a resurrection of the righteous at the time of His Second Coming. These will be people who have earned celestial glory.

1 Corinthians 15:23

23 But every man in his own order [there is an order to the resurrection]: Christ the firstfruits [Christ is the first to be resurrected on this earth]; afterward they [the righteous] that are Christ's at his coming [the Second Coming].

The Doctrine and Covenants tells us that the righteous, whose bodies are still in the grave, will be resurrected and caught up to meet the coming Lord. They will then actually descend to earth with Him as He comes to begin His millennial reign.

D&C 88:97–98

97 And they [the righteous] who have slept in their graves [who have already died] shall come forth, for **their graves shall be opened; and they also shall be caught up to meet him** in the midst of the pillar of heaven—

98 They are Christ's [referring to the righteous Saints, both living (v. 96) and dead (v. 97) who will be caught up to meet the coming Christ], the first fruits, they who shall descend with him first, and they who are on the earth and in their graves, who are first caught up to meet him; and all this by the voice of the sounding of the trump of the angel of God.

Q: We are told that there is an "order" to the resurrection of the dead. Who is resurrected when?

A: There are four major categories of resurrection and five major resurrections spoken of in scripture.

The four major categories of resurrection are:
1. Celestial
2. Terrestrial
3. Telestial
4. Sons of perdition

The five major resurrections are:
1. The resurrection of celestial-quality people at the time of Christ's resurrection.
2. The resurrection of celestial-quality people at the Second Coming (sometimes referred to as the "morning of the first resurrection").
3. The resurrection of the terrestrial-quality people after the righteous are resurrected, near the beginning of the Millennium (sometimes referred to as the "afternoon of the first resurrection"; see *Doctrines of the Gospel Student Manual*, 88).
4. The resurrection of those who led a telestial life. This involves all those from the time of Adam and Eve and takes place after the thousand years of the Millennium have ended (see D&C 88:100–101).
5. The sons of perdition, who are resurrected after the telestial resurrection (D&C 88:102).

In summary, the righteous from Adam to Christ were resurrected with the Savior (see D&C 133:54–55). This was the first group to be resurrected and consisted only of those who are worthy of celestial glory. This group would have included Adam and Eve as well as John the Baptist. The second major resurrection will be the righteous who have died since the Savior's Resurrection

(D&C 88:97–98). They will be resurrected at the beginning of the Millennium with the exception of Peter, James, and Moroni, who are already resurrected. The third major group will be those who lived terrestrial-quality lives since the time of Adam (see D&C 88:99). The fourth group will be those worthy of telestial glory. They will come forth at the end of the Millennium (see D&C 88:100–101). The fifth group, sons of perdition, comes forth at the end of the Millennium, after the telestials are resurrected (see D&C 88:102).

Q: Will there be differences between the resurrected bodies of celestials, terrestrials, telestials, and sons of perdition?

A: Yes.

Paul taught this clearly in 1 Corinthians. Speaking of the resurrection of the dead, he said:

1 Corinthians 15:39–42

39 All flesh is not the same flesh: but there is one kind of flesh of men, another flesh of beasts, another of fishes, and another of birds.

40 There are also **celestial bodies,** and bodies **terrestrial:** but **the glory of the celestial is one, and the glory of the terrestrial is another.**

41 There is one glory of the **sun** [symbolic of celestial glory], and another glory of the **moon** [symbolic of terrestrial glory], and another glory of the **stars** [symbolic of telestial glory]: for **one star differeth from another star in glory.**

42 **So also is the resurrection of the dead.** It is sown in corruption; it is raised in incorruption:

The Lord teaches us the same doctrine in the Doctrine and Covenants:

D&C 88:28–32

28 They who are of a **celestial spirit** [those who live worthy of celestial glory] shall **receive the same body which was a natural body;** even ye shall receive your bodies, and your glory shall be that glory by which your bodies are quickened [resurrected].

29 Ye who are quickened by a portion of the celestial glory shall then receive of the same, even a fulness [of the celestial glory and blessings and privileges].

30 And they who are quickened by a portion of the terrestrial glory [those who are resurrected into terrestrial glory] shall then receive of the same [the terrestrial kingdom], even a fulness [a terrestrial body; note that this verse does not say a "natural body" or "your bodies" as was the case for celestials in verse 28. In other words, a terrestrial body differs from a celestial body.]

31 And also they who are quickened by a portion of the telestial glory shall then receive of the same [the telestial kingdom], even a fulness [all the blessings and privileges, along with the limitations of telestial glory and telestial bodies].

32 And **they who remain** [sons of perdition] shall also be quickened [resurrected]; nevertheless, they shall return again to their own place [outer darkness], to enjoy that which they are willing to receive, because they were not willing to enjoy that which they might have received.

Joseph Fielding Smith gave us additional information concerning the differences in bodies that will exist between those in the different kingdoms of glory.

Joseph Fielding Smith

"In the resurrection there will be **different kinds of bodies.** . . . The body a man receives [in the resurrection] will determine his place hereafter. . . . There will be several classes of resurrected bodies; some **celestial,** some **terrestrial,** some **telestial,** and some **sons of perdition.** Each of these classes will *differ* from the others by *prominent* and *marked distinctions;'* . . . *Celestial bodies* . . . will shine like the sun as our Savior's does. . . . Terrestrial bodies . . . will not shine like the sun, but they will be more glorious than the bodies of those who receive the telestial glory. . . .

"*In both of these kingdoms* [terrestrial and telestial] *there will be changes in the bodies and limitations. They will not have the power of increase, neither the power or nature to live as husbands and wives, for this will be denied them and they cannot increase.*

"Those who receive the exaltation in the celestial kingdom will have the 'continuation of the seeds forever' (D&C 132:19*). They will live in the family relationship.* In the terrestrial and in the telestial kingdoms there will be no marriage. Those who enter there will remain 'separately and singly' [D&C 132:15–32] forever" (*Doctrines of Salvation,* 2:287).

Q: Is it true that resurrection is a priesthood ordinance?
A: Yes.

Brigham Young

"It is supposed by this people that we have all the ordinances in our possession for life and salvation, and exaltation, and that we are administering these ordinances. This is not the case. We are in possession of all the ordinances that can be administered in the flesh; but there are other ordinances and administrations that must be administered beyond this world. I know you would ask what they are. I will mention one. We have not, neither can we receive here, the ordinance and the keys of the resurrection. They will be given to those who have passed off this stage of action and have received their bodies again, as many have already done and many more will. They will be ordained, by those who hold the keys of the resurrection, to go forth and resurrect the Saints just as we receive the ordinance of baptism, then the keys of authority to baptize others for the remission of their sins. This is one of the ordinances we cannot receive here, and there are many more" (*Discourses of Brigham Young*, 397–98).

"Then angels will come and begin to resurrect the dead, and the Savior will also raise the dead, and they [the worthy men who were dead] will receive the keys of the resurrection, and will begin to assist in that work" (*Discourses of Brigham Young*, 115).

"Some person holding the keys of the resurrection, having previously passed through that ordeal, will be delegated to resurrect our bodies, and our spirits will be there and prepared to enter into their bodies" (*Discourses of Brigham Young*, 373).

Spencer W. Kimball

"Today you or I could not stand here and call to life a dead person. But, the day will come when I can take my wife by the hand and raise her out of the grave in the resurrection. The day will come when you can bring each of your family who has preceded you in death back into a resurrected being, to live forever" (Manchester England Area Conference, June 21, 1976).

CHAPTER NINE

THE MILLENNIUM

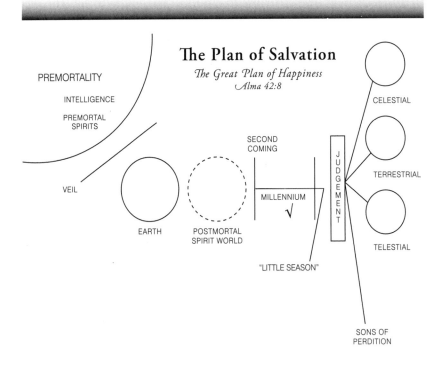

The Plan of Salvation
The Great Plan of Happiness
Alma 42:8

PREMORTALITY

INTELLIGENCE

PREMORTAL
SPIRITS

CELESTIAL

VEIL

SECOND
COMING

JUDGEMENT

TERRESTRIAL

MILLENNIUM
√

EARTH

POSTMORTAL
SPIRIT WORLD

TELESTIAL

"LITTLE SEASON"

SONS OF
PERDITION

We are taught in numerous places in the scriptures that the resurrected Christ will come to rule and reign on the earth for a thousand years. This period is referred to as the Millennium. It will be a time of peace and great accomplishment in the work of saving souls. Untold billions will be born and raised in righteousness, living with Christ as "Lord of lords and King of kings" (Revelation 17:14). The government of the earth during the Millennium will be a theocracy, which means government by God. Christ will be the head of this government. In vision, John the Revelator saw this period of time and the righteous, resurrected Saints who "lived and reigned with Christ a thousand years" (Revelation 20:4). We will ask some questions and provide some answers as we study this stage of the Plan of Salvation.

Q: When does the Millennium begin?

A: When the Savior returns at His Second Coming.

The Doctrine and Covenants teaches this as follows (**bold** added for emphasis):

D&C 29:9–10

9 For the hour is nigh [the Second Coming is near] and the day soon at hand when the earth is ripe; and all the proud and they that do wickedly shall be as stubble; and I will burn them up, saith the Lord of Hosts, that wickedness shall not be upon the earth;

10 For the hour is nigh, and that which was spoken by mine apostles must be fulfilled; for as they spoke so shall it come to pass.

This is also taught in the student manual prepared by the Church for the institutes of religion:

Doctrines of the Gospel Student Manual
"The thousand years of the Millennium will be ushered in when the Savior comes in power and glory" (231–32, 103).

Q: How long will the Millennium last?

A: One thousand years.

D&C 29:11

11 **For I will reveal myself from heaven with power and great glory,** with all the hosts thereof, **and dwell in righteousness with men on earth a thousand years,** and the wicked shall not stand (see also Revelation 20:4).

Q: Will the resurrected Saints who reign with the Savior actually dwell on earth (Revelation 20:6)?

A: Probably not, in the sense of remaining permanently on earth during the entire thousand years. They will be coming and going as needed here and will be continuing to progress toward celestial exaltation themselves.

Joseph Smith

"Christ and the resurrected saints will reign over the earth during the thousand years. They will not probably dwell upon the earth, but will visit it when they please or when it is necessary to govern it" (*Teachings of the Prophet Joseph Smith*, 268).

President Brigham Young taught the same thing, with a bit more detail:

Brigham Young

"Do you know that it is the eleventh hour of the reign of Satan on the earth? **Jesus is coming to reign,** and all you who fear and tremble because of your enemies, cease to fear them, and learn to fear to offend God, fear to transgress his laws, fear to do any evil to your brother, or to any being upon the earth, and do not fear Satan and his power, nor those who have only power to slay the body, for God will preserve his people.

"In the progress of the age in which we live, we discern the fulfillment of prophecy, and the preparation for the second coming of our Lord and Savior to dwell upon the earth. We expect that the refuge of lies will be swept away, and that city, nation, government, or kingdom which serves not God, and gives no heed to the principles of truth and religion, will be utterly wasted away and destroyed.

"Jesus has been upon the earth a great many more times than you are aware of. When Jesus makes his next appearance upon the earth, but few of this Church will be prepared to receive him and see him face to face and converse with him; but he will come to his temple. **Will he remain and dwell upon the earth a thousand years, without returning? He will come here, and return to his mansions where he dwells with his Father, and come again to the earth, and again return to his Father,** according to my understanding" (*Discourses of Brigham Young,* 114–15).

Q: Will Satan be bound during the Millennium so that he can't tempt people, or will people ignore his temptations?

A: He will not be allowed to tempt.

In attempting to answer this question, some people refer to 1 Nephi 22:26 to support the idea that Satan will be around during the Millennium tempting people but that people will "bind" him by ignoring him. Others use D&C 101:28 to conclude that Satan will not be allowed to tempt at all during the Millennium. We will quote both of these references here and then support the answer given above. Both references refer to the Millennium.

1 Nephi 22:26

26 And because of the righteousness of his people, Satan has no power; wherefore, he cannot be loosed for the space of many years; for he hath no power over the hearts of the people, for they dwell in righteousness, and the Holy One of Israel reigneth.

D&C 101:28

28 And in that day Satan shall not have power to tempt any man.

This is one of those situations in the scriptures in which we need to think through the issues and then see what other scriptural references as well as the Brethren have said before we come to a final conclusion ourselves. For instance, the book of Revelation provides additional insights to this issue in the following verses:

Revelation 20:1–3

1 And I saw an angel come down from heaven, **having the key** [priesthood key, given by God] of the bottomless pit **and a great chain** in his hand [symbolic of power to bind Satan and keep him from tempting].

2 And he laid hold on the dragon, that old serpent, which is the Devil, and Satan, and **bound him a thousand years,**

3 And cast him into the bottomless pit, and **shut him up,** and **set a seal upon him,** that he should **deceive the nations no more,** till the thousand years should be fulfilled: and after that he must be loosed a little season.

In a sense, we can bind Satan by personal righteousness and by refusing his temptations, but we do not have power to stop him from trying to tempt. Christ, however, does have that power. Thus, He will bind him—stop him from tempting during the Millennium. Joseph Fielding Smith is quoted on this issue in the *Doctrine and Covenants Student Manual* as follows:

Joseph Fielding Smith

"There are many among us who **teach** that **the binding of Satan will be merely** the binding which those dwelling on the earth will place upon him **by their refusal to hear his enticings. This is not so. He will not have the privilege during that period of time to tempt any man** (D&C 101:28)" (*Church History and Modern Revelation*, 1:192; see *also Doctrine and Covenants Student Manual*, 89).

Q: Will there be any people besides Latter-day Saints on earth during the Millennium?
A: Yes.

Joseph Fielding Smith

"There will be millions of people, Catholics, Protestants, agnostics, Mohammedans, people of all classes, and of all beliefs, still permitted to remain upon the face of the earth, but they will be those who have lived clean lives, those who have been free from wickedness and corruption. All who belong, by virtue of their good lives, to the terrestrial order, as well as those who have kept the celestial law, will remain upon the face of the earth during the millennium" (*Doctrines of Salvation*, 1:86).

Q: What will daily life be like during the Millennium?

A: Similar to the good aspects of life we enjoy now but with major enhancements.

Bruce R. McConkie

"During the millennial era, . . . mortality as such will continue. Children will be born, grow up, marry, advance to old age, and pass through the equivalent of death. Crops will be planted, harvested, and eaten; industries will be expanded, cities built, and education fostered; men will continue to care for their own needs, handle their own affairs, and enjoy the full endowment of free agency. Speaking a pure language (Zeph. 3:9), dwelling in peace, living without disease, and progressing as the Holy Spirit will guide, the advancement and perfection of society during the millennium will exceed anything men have supposed or expected" (*Mormon Doctrine*, 496–97).

Joseph Fielding Smith

"'And in that day whatsoever any man shall ask, it shall be given unto him. And in that day Satan shall not have power to tempt any man. And there shall be no sorrow because there is no death. In that day an infant shall not die until he is old; and his life shall be as the age of a tree; and when he dies he shall not sleep, that is to say in the earth, but shall be changed in the twinkling of an eye, and shall be caught up, and his rest shall be glorious' [D&C 101: 27–31].

"**That will be a glorious day.** It is not a day to be dreaded by those who are righteous, but it is a day, *a dreadful day, unto the wicked*, . . . for *all who will not put themselves in harmony with the gospel of Jesus Christ and with his everlasting truth, and have in their hearts peace, shall be consumed.*

"It shall be in that day that the lion shall lie down with

the lamb and eat straw as the ox, and all fear, hatred, and enmity shall depart from the earth because *all things having hate in their hearts shall pass away;* and there shall come a change, a *change over men, a change over the beasts* of the field, and upon *all* things living upon the face of the earth.

"According to this word I have read there shall be harmony, and love, and peace, and righteousness because Satan is bound that he cannot tempt any man, and that will be the condition that shall be upon the earth for 1,000 years. Not only that, but men shall live *free from sin* and *free from the ravages of disease* and *death* until they reach the age of 100 years. Infants shall not die, they shall live until they have filled the measure of their mortal creation. In fact, mortality shall be reduced to a minimum" (*Doctrines of Salvation,* 3:57–58).

Q: How old will mortals live to be during the Millennium?

A: One hundred years.

The "age of a tree" is the most common scriptural answer when referring to the age of people during the Millennium (see D&C 101:30). The problem is that we don't know what kind of a tree, but Isaiah solves this dilemma by telling us that mortals on earth during the Millennium will live to be one hundred years old (Isaiah 65:20):

Isaiah 65:20
20 There shall be no more thence an infant of days, nor an old man that hath not filled his days: for the child shall die an hundred years old; but the sinner being **an hundred years old** shall be accursed.

The following quote also helps answer the question:

Doctrines of the Gospel Student Manual

"Men shall die when they are one hundred years of age, and the change shall be made suddenly to the immortal state. . . . In the Millennium children will grow up and live upon the earth until they are one hundred years old (see Isaiah 65:20; D&C 101:29–31; 63:50–51; 45:58)."

Q: Is it true that righteous mothers will get to raise their little children who have died?

A: Yes.

Joseph F. Smith

"Joseph Smith declared that the mother who laid down her little child, being deprived of the privilege, the joy, and the satisfaction of bringing it up to manhood or womanhood in this world, would, after the resurrection, have all the joy, satisfaction and pleasure, and even more than it would have been possible to have had in mortality, in seeing her child grow to the full measure of the stature of its spirit. . . . When the mother is deprived of the pleasure and joy of rearing her babe to manhood or to womanhood in this life, through the hand of death, that privilege will be renewed to her hereafter, and she will enjoy it to a fuller fruition than it would be possible for her to do here. When she does it there, it will be with the certain knowledge that the results will be without fail" (*Gospel Doctrine*, 453, 454).

Q: Will righteous fathers have the same privilege?

A: Yes. They will raise these children with their wives.

We get a clue to this answer from the fact that raising children beyond the veil is done by both a mother and a father. Joseph

Fielding Smith taught that righteous "parents" (a team) will have their children in the next life:

Joseph Fielding Smith

"If parents are righteous, they will have their children after the resurrection. Little children who die, whose parents are not worthy of an exaltation, will be *adopted* into the families of those who are worthy" (*Doctrines of Salvation*, 2:56).

Q: What happens to stillborn children?
A: They will be raised in the resurrection also.

Encyclopedia of Mormonism

"Although temple ordinances are not performed for stillborn children, no loss of eternal blessings or family unity is implied. The family may record the name of a stillborn child on the family group record followed by the word stillborn in parentheses" (see "stillborn").

Church Handbook of Instructions

"Temple ordinances are not performed for stillborn children, but no loss of eternal blessings or family unity is implied. The family may record the name of a stillborn child on the family group record followed by the word stillborn in parentheses" (76).

Bruce R. McConkie

"The spirit enters the body at the time of quickening, months prior to the actual normal birth. The value and comfort attending a knowledge of this eternal truth is seen in connection with stillborn children. Since the spirit entered the body before birth, stillborn children will be resurrected and righteous parents shall enjoy their association in immortal glory" (*Doctrinal New Testament Commentary*, 84–85).

Q: What about miscarriages or babies who are aborted?

A: We don't know. The Lord has not yet revealed the answer.

Q: When a baby dies, is it a baby or an adult in the post-mortal spirit world?

A: It is a full-grown adult.

Joseph Fielding Smith

"When a baby dies, it goes back into the spirit world, and the spirit assumes its natural form as an adult, for we were all adults before we were born.

"When a child is raised in the resurrection, that spirit will enter the body and the body will be the same size as it was when the child died. It will then grow after the resurrection to full maturity to conform to the size of the spirit (*Doctrines of Salvation*, 2:56).

Q: Will mortals actually die during the Millennium after they've lived to be a hundred years old?

A: Yes.

They will die but will be immediately resurrected.

D&C 101:31

"And when he dies he shall not sleep, that is to say in the earth, but shall be changed in the twinkling of an eye, and shall be caught up and his rest shall be glorious" (D&C 101:31).

Q: What is the major purpose of the Millennium?

A: Temple work.

Work for the dead is the crowning work of the Millennium. The fact that a thousand years is needed indicates that there will be a great deal of success in saving the dead.

As the thousand-year Millennium draws to a close, a great, final battle looms. It will be the final scene in what started as the War in Heaven. We will consider this in the next chapter.

CHAPTER TEN

THE BATTLE OF GOG AND MAGOG

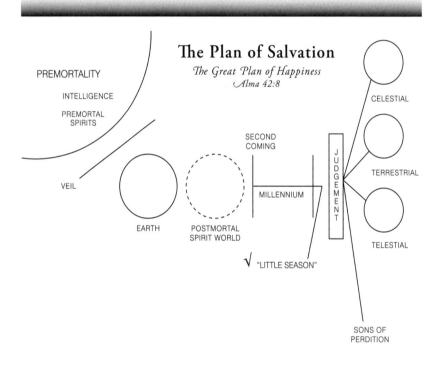

The Plan of Salvation
The Great Plan of Happiness
Alma 42:8

PREMORTALITY

INTELLIGENCE

PREMORTAL
SPIRITS

VEIL

EARTH

POSTMORTAL
SPIRIT WORLD

SECOND
COMING

MILLENNIUM

"LITTLE SEASON"

JUDGEMENT

CELESTIAL

TERRESTRIAL

TELESTIAL

SONS OF
PERDITION

The took of Revelation mentions "Gog and Magog" in conjunction with the loosing of Satan at the end of the Millennium:

Revelation 20:7–8

7 And when the thousand years are expired, Satan shall be loosed out of his prison,

8 And shall go out to deceive the nations which are in the four quarters of the earth, **Gog and Magog,** to gather them together to battle: the number of whom is as the sand of the sea.

Q: What happens at the end of the Millennium?

A: Satan and his evil hosts will be let loose for a "little season," and the Battle of Gog and Magog will take place (D&C 88:111–15).

Many mortals on earth at the end of the Millennium will reject the Savior, whom they know, and will reject His millennial ministry and turn to wickedness. The end of the war that began in heaven, usually referred to as the battle of Gog and Magog, will take place (see "Gog" in Bible Dictionary). Michael (Adam) will gather the armies of righteousness, and the devil will gather his armies of evil. The devil and his "hosts of hell" will be defeated and then cast out forever (D&C 88:111–15).

CHAPTER ELEVEN

FINAL JUDGMENT CATEGORIES:
QUALIFICATIONS FOR THE THREE DEGREES OF GLORY AND PERDITION

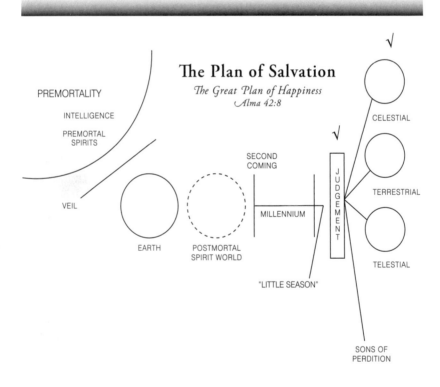

The Plan of Salvation
The Great Plan of Happiness
Alma 42:8

PREMORTALITY

INTELLIGENCE

PREMORTAL SPIRITS

VEIL

EARTH

POSTMORTAL SPIRIT WORLD

SECOND COMING

MILLENNIUM

"LITTLE SEASON"

JUDGEMENT

CELESTIAL

TERRESTRIAL

TELESTIAL

SONS OF PERDITION

We now come to "final judgment." Perhaps you've noticed that there have been several other "judgment days" along the course of the Plan of Salvation. For example, there was a judgment day in premortality that determined whether we went with Satan (as he was cast out of heaven) or were to be allowed to be born on earth and continue our education and growth toward exaltation. There is another judgment at the time of our physical death that determines whether we go to paradise or spirit prison. There is yet another judgment at the time we are resurrected. If we get resurrected into a telestial body, for instance, we know we are going to the telestial kingdom. If we get a celestial body at the time of our resurrection, we know we are going to celestial glory. See Doctrine and Covenants 88:28–32, which explains this doctrine for the three degrees of glory and perdition. With these various judgments in mind, we can better understand the significance of the "final judgment," which will take place after the Millennium is over and after the "little season."

The book of Revelation speaks of this final judgment as follows:

Revelation 20:12

12 And I saw the dead, small and great, stand before God; and the books were opened: and another book was opened, which is the book of life: and the dead were judged out of those things which were written in the books, according to their works.

The four major categories to which people may be assigned on the final Judgment Day, beginning with the lowest, are:
1. Sons of perdition
2. Telestial glory
3. Terrestrial glory
4. Celestial glory (exaltation)

We will take a brief look at the qualifications for each of the degrees of glory and for perdition (or "outer darkness," as it is often referred to by members of the Church), relying heavily on

Doctrine and Covenants section 76, with **bold** added for emphasis.

Sons of Perdition (Outer Darkness)

Those who become sons of perdition must meet certain qualifications:

1. They must **"know my [God's] power"** (D&C 76:31).

In order to "know" God and His power, one must have a witness of the Holy Ghost concerning God and His power. Joseph Smith taught as follows:

Joseph Smith

"What must a man do to commit the unpardonable sin? He must receive the Holy Ghost, have the heavens opened unto him, and know God, and then sin against Him. After a man has sinned against the Holy Ghost, there is no repentance for him. He has got to say that the sun does not shine while he sees it; he has got to deny Jesus Christ when the heavens have been opened unto him, and to deny the plan of salvation with his eyes open to the truth of it; and from that time he begins to be an enemy. This is the case with many apostates of the Church of Jesus Christ of Latter-day Saints" *(Teachings of the Prophet Joseph Smith, 358).*

2. They must **"have been made partakers"** of God's power (D&C 76:31).

They are members of the Church and have received all of the ordinances, endowments, and so forth made available on earth to prepare for exaltation. Joseph F. Smith declared:

Joseph Fielding Smith

"And he that believes, is baptized, and receives the light and testimony of Jesus Christ . . . **receiving the fullness of the blessings of the gospel in this world, and after-**

wards turns wholly unto sin, violating his covenants . . . will taste the second death" (*Gospel Doctrine*, 476–77).

3. They must have **"suffered themselves** [allowed themselves through agency choices] through the power of the devil **to be overcome"** (D&C 76:31).

In other words, they must intentionally allow themselves to be overcome by Satan.

4. They must **"deny the truth"** (D&C 76:31).

They become complete liars, lacking all integrity; in other words, they become totally dishonest, just like Satan, denying the truth when they fully know it.

5. They must **"defy my power"** (D&C 76:31).

They don't just go inactive, but they fight against God, the Church, and all that is good with the same evil energy that Satan and his hosts use to fight truth and right.

6. They must become **" vessels of wrath"** (D&C 76:33).

They become full of anger, bitterness, and hate against that which is good. In other words, they actually become like Satan. They think as he does, act as he does, and react against good just as he does. This is the full opposite of becoming like Christ by following His commandments and living His gospel.

7. They must have **"crucified him** [Christ] **unto themselves and put him to an open shame"** (D&C 76:35).

They become so bitter that they would gladly crucify Christ themselves if they had the opportunity. In other words, they have become like Satan. They think as he does, hate as he does, and have the same desires and goals as he does. President Brigham Young summarized the process of becoming sons of perdition as follows:

Brigham Young

"How much does it take to prepare a man, or woman . . . to become angels to the devil, to suffer with him through all eternity? Just as much as it does to prepare a man to go into the Celestial Kingdom, into the presence of the Father and the Son, and to be made an heir to his kingdom and all his glory, and be crowned with crowns of glory, immortality, and eternal lives" (in *Journal of Discourses*, 3:93).

Q: Do sons of perdition get resurrected?

A: Yes, if you are referring to mortals who becomes sons of perdition. No, if you are thinking of the evil spirits who were cast out with Lucifer during the War in Heaven. They did not qualify to receive physical bodies; therefore, they will not be resurrected.

All who have ever been born (received mortal, physical bodies) on this earth will be resurrected, regardless of how they lived their lives. We will quote one of many scriptural passages to this effect:

D&C 29:26

26 But, behold, verily I say unto you, before the earth shall pass away, Michael, mine archangel, shall sound his trump, and then shall all the dead awake, for their graves shall be opened, and they shall come forth—yea, **even all.**

Q: Can women become daughters of perdition?

A: Some say yes; some say no.

This question has been debated by many. Some suggest that women are not capable of becoming evil enough. Others feel that they are capable. Some believe that becoming a son of perdition requires ordination to the Melchizedek Priesthood. Others believe that the only qualification is that of having a sure testimony, given by the Holy Ghost, which both men and women can have.

The term "sons of" is often used in the scriptures to mean "followers of" and has nothing to do with gender in most such contexts. A strong argument in favor of women qualifying to become sons of perdition is the fact that they, like men, can achieve exaltation and become gods (see D&C 132:20). Therefore, it would seem logical that they could obtain the lowest reward as well. As quoted above, President Young asked, "How much does it take to prepare **a man, or woman,** . . . to become angels to the devil [sons of perdition], to suffer with him through all eternity?" (*Journal of Discourses*, 3:93).

Telestial Glory

Briefly put, those who qualify for telestial glory are liars, sorcerers, adulterers, whoremongers, and murderers (see Revelation 22:15; D&C 76:81–89, 98–103).

D&C 76:81–89

81 And again, we saw the glory of the **telestial,** which glory is that of the lesser, even as the glory of the stars differs from that of the glory of the moon in the firmament.

82 These are they who **received not the gospel of Christ** [refused to accept it and make it part of their lives when given opportunities to do so], neither the testimony of Jesus.

83 These are they who **deny not the Holy Spirit** [they are not sons of perdition].

84 These are they who are **thrust down to hell** [they will be turned over to Satan during the Millennium to pay for their sins; see D&C 19:15–17].

85 These are they who **shall not be redeemed from the devil until the last resurrection** [they will not be resurrected until the end of the Millennium; see D&C 88:100–101], until the Lord, even Christ the lamb, shall have finished his work.

86 These are they who **receive not of his fulness in the eternal world** [they will not receive the blessings of celestial glory, including the privilege of living with the Father and the Son], but of the Holy Ghost [they will be visited by the Holy Ghost] through the ministration of the terrestrial [people from the terrestrial glory can visit the telestial glory];

87 And the terrestrial through the ministration of the celestial [people from celestial glory can visit the terrestrial kingdom].

88 And also **the telestial receive it of the administering of angels** who are appointed to minister for them, or who are appointed to be **ministering spirits for them;** for **they shall be heirs of salvation** [they get a certain degree of "salvation" and will be out of reach of Satan forever].

89 And thus we saw, in the heavenly vision, **the glory of the telestial,** which **surpasses all understanding** [the telestial kingdom is glorious beyond our ability to imagine—a reminder that the Lord is merciful and kind].

D&C 76:98–103

98 And the glory of the **telestial** is one [of the categories of glory], even as the glory of the stars is one; for **as one star differs from another star in glory, even so differs one from another in glory in the telestial world.**

99 For these are they who are of Paul, and of Apollos, and of Cephas.

100 These are they who say they are some of one and some of another—some of Christ and some of John, and some of Moses, and some of Elias, and some of Esaias, and some of Isaiah, and some of Enoch [these include those who accept one prophet but not another];

101 But **received not the gospel,** neither **the testimony of Jesus,** neither **the prophets,** neither **the everlasting gospel.**

102 Last of all, **these all are they who will not be gathered with the saints, to be caught up unto the church of the Firstborn** [they will not be caught up to meet the Savior when he comes in clouds of glory; see D&C 88:96–97], **and received into the cloud.**

103 These are they who are **liars,** and **sorcerers,** and **adulterers,** and **whoremongers** [people who make illicit sex the central focus of their lives], and **whosoever loves and makes a lie.**

A false rumor continues to be passed around to the effect that the Prophet Joseph Smith once said that if we knew how beautiful the telestial kingdom is, we would commit suicide to get there. This is not true. Knowing what we do about telestial glory, just imagine what it will be like to receive celestial glory and exaltation!

Perhaps you have noticed that by far the majority of God's teachings to us through the scriptures and the prophets consists of instructions for obtaining the celestial kingdom and avoiding telestial sins. The terrestrial kingdom and sons of perdition are rarely spoken of, as is the case with the lower two levels of the celestial kingdom. The message, then, is obvious: our Father in Heaven wants us to train our sights on celestial exaltation and avoid the debilitating effects of telestial living.

Terrestrial Glory

The terrestrial glory consists of those who die without law. They are good and honorable people who do not accept the gospel in this life when given plenty of opportunities but decide to accept it in the spirit world. This kingdom will include Latter-day Saints who are not valiant in living according to their testimonies.

D&C 76:71–79

71 And again, we saw the **terrestrial** world, and behold and lo, these are they who are of the terrestrial, whose **glory differs** from that of the church of the First-born [those who receive exaltation in the highest degree in celestial glory] who have received the fulness of the Father, **even as that of the moon differs from the sun** in the firmament.

72 Behold, these are **they who died without law** [who refused to accept the gospel when given the opportunity in the spirit prison]; **[Author: this verse seems to apply to those who "died" without law, meaning that they didn't accept the gospel while on earth]**

73 And also they who are spirits of men kept in prison, whom the Son visited, and preached the gospel to them, that they might be judged according to men in the flesh;

74 Who **received not the testimony of Jesus in the flesh, but afterwards** [in spirit prison] **received it.**

75 These are they who are **honorable men** of the earth, who were **blinded by the craftiness of men.**

76 These are they who **receive of his glory, but not of his fullness** [not the full blessings of celestial glory and exaltation].

77 These are they who **receive of the presence of the Son,** but **not of the fullness of the Father.**

78 Wherefore, they are **bodies terrestrial,** and **not bodies celestial,** and **differ in glory as the moon differs from the sun.**

79 These are they who are **not valiant in the testimony of Jesus;** wherefore, they obtain not the crown over the kingdom of our God.

Celestial Glory

Inheritors of celestial glory are faithful, baptized members of the Church who have the gift of the Holy Ghost and strive to keep the commandments, thus qualifying to be "washed and cleansed from all their sins."

D&C 76:50–70

50 And again we bear record—for we saw and heard, and this is the testimony of the gospel of Jesus Christ concerning them who **shall come forth in the resurrection of the just** [the resurrection of the righteous]—

51 They are they who **received the testimony of Jesus,** and **believed on his name** and **were baptized** after the manner of his burial, being buried in the water in his name, and this according to the commandment which he has given—

52 That by **keeping the commandments** they might be **washed and cleansed from all their sins,** and **receive the Holy Ghost** by the laying on of the hands of him who is ordained and sealed to this power;

53 And **overcome by faith,** and are **sealed by the Holy Spirit of promise,** which the Father sheds forth upon all those who are just and true.

54 They are they who are **the church of the First-born.**

55 They are they into whose hands the Father has **given all things—**

56 They are they who are priests and kings, who have **received of his fullness, and of his glory;**

57 And **are priests of the Most High, after the order of Melchizedek,** which was after the order of Enoch, which was after the order of the Only Begotten Son.

58 Wherefore, as it is written, **they are gods,** even the sons of God—

59 Wherefore, **all things are theirs,** whether life or

death, or things present, or things to come, all are theirs and **they are Christ's,** and Christ is God's.

60 And **they shall overcome all things.**

61 Wherefore, let no man glory in man, but rather let him glory in God, who shall subdue all enemies under his feet.

62 These shall **dwell in the presence of God and his Christ forever and ever.**

63 These are **they whom he shall bring with him, when he shall come in the clouds of heaven** to reign on the earth over his people.

64 These are they who **shall have part in the first resurrection.**

65 These are they who **shall come forth in the resurrection of the just.**

66 These are they who are come unto Mount Zion [the New Jerusalem; see D&C 84:2], and unto the city of the living God, the heavenly place, the holiest of all.

67 These are they who have come to an **innumerable** [many people will attain celestial exaltation] company of angels, to the general assembly and church of Enoch [an another name for exaltation], and of the Firstborn.

68 These are they **whose names are written in heaven** [in the "book of life"; see Revelation 3:5], where God and Christ are the judge of all.

69 These are they who are **just men made perfect through Jesus** the mediator of the new covenant, who wrought out this perfect atonement through the shedding of his own blood.

70 These are they whose **bodies are celestial,** whose **glory is that of the sun,** even the glory of God, **the highest of all,** whose glory the sun of the firmament is written of as being typical.

Exaltation

Those who are exalted are faithful Church members who, in addition to fulfilling the other requirements for attaining celestial glory, are endowed and married in the temple—sealed as husband and wife by the Holy Spirit of Promise (the Holy Ghost), as stated in D&C 132:19. They attain the highest degree of the celestial kingdom, becoming gods and living as families forever (D&C 131:1–4; 132:19–20).

Exaltation is described in the following verses:

D&C 131:1–4

1 **In the celestial glory there are three heavens or degrees;**

2 And in order to obtain the **highest,** a man must enter into this order of the priesthood [meaning the new and everlasting covenant of **marriage**];

3 And if he does not, he cannot obtain it.

4 He may enter into the other [the lower two categories of the celestial kingdom], but that is the end of his kingdom; he cannot have an increase [live with his family and have children].

D&C 132: 19–20

19 And again, verily I say unto you, if a man **marry** a wife **by my word,** which is **my law,** and by the **new and everlasting covenant,** and it is **sealed** unto them **by the Holy Spirit of promise** [ratified by the Holy Ghost; in other words, no one can sneak by], **by him who is anointed, unto whom I have appointed this power and the keys of this priesthood;** and it shall be said unto them—Ye shall come forth in the first resurrection; and if it be after the first resurrection, in the next resurrection; and **shall inherit thrones, kingdoms, principalities, and powers, dominions, all heights and depths**—then shall it be written in the Lamb's Book of Life, that he shall

commit no murder whereby to shed innocent blood, and if ye abide in my covenant, and commit no murder whereby to shed innocent blood [if they shall commit no unforgivable sin, and if they repent properly for the sins they commit], it shall be done unto them in all things whatsoever my servant hath put upon them, in time, and through all eternity; and shall be of full force when they are out of the world; and they shall **pass by the angels, and the gods,** which are set there, **to their exaltation** and glory in all things, as hath been sealed upon their heads, which glory shall be **a continuation of the seeds forever and ever** [they shall have spirit children forever in a family unit].

20 **Then shall they** [the husband and wife] **be gods,** because they have no end; therefore shall they be from everlasting to everlasting, because they continue; **then shall they be above all,** because **all things are subject unto them. Then shall they be gods,** because **they have all power,** and the **angels are subject to them.**

Note that verse 20 above is a description of the powers that our Heavenly Father has. We will now ask a few more questions:

Q: Will all people be separate and single except those who attain exaltation?

A: Yes (see D&C 131:1–4; 132:15–32).

The following quote from Joseph Fielding Smith explains this:

Joseph Fielding Smith
"In the terrestrial and in the telestial kingdoms there will be no marriage. Those who enter there will remain 'separately and singly' forever [see D&C 132:15–32]" (*Doctrines of Salvation*, 2:287).

Q: What happens to the righteous who wanted to marry but died without getting a fair chance to do so in mortality?

A: All people will have a completely fair chance to marry for time and eternity, either in this life or through missionary work in the spirit world and ordinances performed for the dead in temples. In other words, all will have a completely fair opportunity for the blessings of eternal marriage before the final judgment.

President Spencer W. Kimball addressed this issue as follows:

Spencer W. Kimball

"We promise you that insofar as eternity is concerned, no soul will be deprived of rich and high and eternal blessings for anything which that person could not help, that the Lord never fails in his promises, and that every righteous person will receive eventually all to which the person is entitled and which he or she has not forfeited through any fault of his or her own" (**[Author: title?]** *Ensign*, October 1979, 50).

Q: After final judgment, can a person progress from one kingdom to another?

A: We don't know.

The position of the First Presidency, as given through the Church Correlation Department to Church curriculum writers, reiterated in 2001, is that we don't have sufficient information from the Lord on this matter to give a final answer at this time.

Q: How long will it be after we die before we are exalted?

A: "A great while."

Joseph Smith

"When you climb up a ladder, you must begin at the bottom, and ascend step by step, until you arrive at the top; and so it is with the principles of the Gospel—you must begin with the first, and go on until you learn all the principles of exaltation. But **it will be a great while after you have passed through the veil** before you will have learned them. It is not all to be comprehended in this world; **it will be a great work to learn our salvation and exaltation even beyond the grave**" (*Teachings of the Prophet Joseph Smith*, 348).

The comforting doctrine in this quote from the Prophet Joseph Smith reminds us that we don't have to be perfect at the time we pass from this life.

Q: Do we, as members of the Church, have to be nearly perfect when we die in order to obtain exaltation on Judgment Day?

A: No. But we do need to be working toward that goal.

Elder Dallin H. Oaks spoke about this subject as follows:

Dallin H. Oaks

"Another idea that is powerful to lift us from discouragement is that the work of the Church . . . is an eternal work. Not all problems . . . are fixed in mortality. The work of salvation goes on beyond the veil of death, and we should not be too apprehensive about incompleteness within the limits of mortality" ("Powerful Ideas," *Ensign*, November 1995, 26).

Elder Marvin J. Ashton also addressed this topic as follows:

Marvin J. Ashton

"It occurs to me that there are probably hundreds or even thousands who do not understand what worthiness is. **Worthiness is a process, and perfection is an eternal trek.** We can be worthy to enjoy certain privileges without being perfect.

"I am also convinced of the fact that the speed with which we head along the straight and narrow path isn't as important as the direction in which we are traveling. That direction, if it is leading toward eternal goals, is the all-important factor" ("On Being Worthy," *Ensign,* May 1989, 21).

Joseph Fielding Smith offered this counsel:

Joseph Fielding Smith

"Salvation does not come all at once; we are commanded to be perfect even as our Father in heaven is perfect. It will take us ages to accomplish this end, for there will be greater progress beyond the grave, and it will be there that the faithful will overcome all things, and receive all things, even the fulness of the Father's glory.

"I believe the Lord meant just what he said: that we should be perfect, as our Father in Heaven is perfect. That will not come all at once, but line upon line, and precept upon precept, example upon example, and even then not as long as we live in this mortal life, for we will have to go even beyond the grave before we reach that perfection and shall be like God" (*Doctrines of Salvation,* 2:18).

Q: If we become gods, will we use the same Plan of Salvation for our own spirit children? (D&C 132:20).

A: Yes.

In 1916 the First Presidency of the Church issued the following statement:

The First Presidency

"Only resurrected and glorified beings can become parents of spirit offspring. Only such exalted souls have reached maturity in the appointed course of eternal life; and the spirits born to them in the eternal worlds will pass in due sequence through the several stages or estates by which the glorified parents have attained exaltation" (First Presidency Statement, *Improvement Era,* August 1916, 942).

Conclusion

In conclusion, an understanding and basic knowledge of the Plan of Salvation is essential for progressing toward exaltation in the highest degree of glory in the celestial kingdom. Those members of the Church who intentionally study these precious doctrines are in a much better position to make wise choices because of the perspective given them by these gospel truths. Such understanding gives the Holy Ghost a much better chance to guide our thoughts and actions. These "points of my doctrine" (D&C 10:62–63) enable us to change or strengthen our behavior as we strive to conform our lives to the gospel of Jesus Christ.

SOURCES

Book of Mormon Student Manual. Salt Lake City: The Church of Jesus Christ of Latter-day Saints (Institutes of Religion), 1979.

Clark, James R., comp. *Messages of the First Presidency of The Church of Jesus Christ of Latter-day Saints.* 6 vols. Salt Lake City: Bookcraft, 1965–75.

Conference Reports of The Church of Jesus Christ of Latter-day Saints. Salt Lake City: The Church of Jesus Christ of Latter-day Saints, 1898 to present.

Doctrine and Covenants Student Manual. Salt Lake City: The Church of Jesus Christ of Latter-day Saints (Institutes of Religion), 1981.

Doctrines of the Gospel Student Manual. Salt Lake City: The Church of Jesus Christ of Latter-day Saints (Institutes of Religion), 1986.

Encyclopedia of Mormonism. Edited by Daniel H. Ludlow. 5 vols. New York: Macmillan, 1992.

Journal of Discourses. 26 vols. London: Latter-day Saints' Book Depot, 1854–86.

Kimball, Spencer W. *The Miracle of Forgiveness.* Salt Lake City: Bookcraft, 1969.

The Life and Teachings of Jesus and His Apostles: New Testament Student Manual. Salt Lake City: The Church of Jesus Christ of

Latter-day Saints, 1979.

McConkie, Bruce R. *Doctrinal New Testament Commentary.* 3 vols. Salt Lake City: Bookcraft, 1965–73.

———. *The Millennial Messiah.* Salt Lake City: Deseret Book, 1982.

———. *Mormon Doctrine.* Salt Lake City: Bookcraft, 1966.

———. *The Mortal Messiah: From Bethlehem to Calvary.* 4 vols. Salt Lake City: Deseret Book, 1979–81.

Old Testament Student Manual. 2 vols. Salt Lake City: The Church of Jesus Christ of Latter-day Saints (Institutes of Religion), 1981.

Pratt, Parley P. *Key to the Science of Theology.* Salt Lake City: Deseret Book, 1979.

Smith, Joseph. *History of The Church of Jesus Christ of Latter-day Saints.* Edited by B. H. Roberts, 2d ed. rev., 7 vols. Salt Lake City: The Church of Jesus Christ of Latter-day Saints, 1932–51.

———. *Teachings of the Prophet Joseph Smith.* Selected by Joseph Fielding Smith. Salt Lake City: Deseret Book, 1976.

Smith, Joseph F. *Gospel Doctrine.* Salt Lake City: Deseret Book, 1939.

Smith, Joseph Fielding. *Answers to Gospel Questions.* Compiled by Joseph Fielding Smith Jr. 5 vols. Salt Lake City: Deseret Book, 1957–66.

———. *Church History and Modern Revelation—A Course of Study for Melchizedek Priesthood Quorums.* Salt Lake City: The Council of the Twelve Apostles of The Church of Jesus Christ of Latter-day Saints, 1946.

―――. *Doctrines of Salvation*. 3 vols. Edited by Bruce R. McConkie. Salt Lake City: Bookcraft, 1954–56.

―――. *The Progress of Man*. Salt Lake City: Deseret Book, 1973.

―――. *Take Heed to Yourselves!* Salt Lake City: Deseret Book, 1966.

―――. *The Way to Perfection*. Salt Lake City: Deseret Book, 1975.

Talmage, James. *The Articles of Faith*. Salt Lake City: Deseret Book, 1984.

―――. *Jesus the Christ*. Salt Lake City: Deseret Book, 1977.

Teachings of Presidents of the Church—Brigham Young. Salt Lake City: The Church of Jesus Christ of Latter-day Saints, 1997.

Widtsoe, John A. *Evidences and Reconciliations*. Salt Lake City: Bookcraft, 1943.

Young, Brigham. *Discourses of Brigham Young*. Selected by John A. Widtsoe. Salt Lake City: Deseret Book, 1954.

ABOUT THE AUTHOR

David J. Ridges taught in the Church Educational System for thirty-five years and has taught for several years at BYU Campus Education Week and Know Your Religion programs. He has also served as a curriculum writer for Sunday School, seminary, and institute of religion manuals.

Brother Ridges has served as a gospel doctrine teacher, bishop, stake president, and patriarch. He is the author of the best-selling Gospel Studies Series books *The Book of Mormon Made Easier, The Doctrine and Covenants Made Easier, The New Testament Made Easier,* and *Isaiah Made Easier.* He is also the author of *50 Signs of the Times and the Second Coming* and *The Proclamation on the Family: The Word of the Lord on More Than 30 Current Issues.*

He and his wife, Janette, live in Springville, Utah. They are the parents of six children.